DAY*care* diaries

"It is such a wonderful feeling knowing that my children love to go to daycare. It is a day filled with friends and fun for them. I appreciate the daily opportunities to talk to my daycare provider about how my children are developing and ask any questions I may have which helps me know if I should or shouldn't be worried about their development. I have total trust during the day that my children are well taken care of by a person that is the closest thing to a surrogate mom who thinks very much like I do regarding children's safety and well-being. I consider our daycare mom to be a "gift from heaven". I respect her great knowledge of children, philosophy of childcare and her practice of keeping kids happy, healthy, and safe by providing fun activities, a clean environment and constant supervision. Our daycare has become a new extension of "family" for us. We feel very blessed and fortunate to have found a daycare provider who's whole family has embraced and opened their home and hearts to us."

—**JLG**

"My kids and I have been blessed to have found a wonderful center. Being a young single Mom, I was very unsure of bringing my boys to a daycare center, especially my infant. I didn't know what to expect and just the feeling of leaving my kids with someone other than family for the first time was a big step. Over the years I can now say I made a great choice! My older son is now 4 and everyday he comes home with a new story about him and his friends. This always makes for a great conversation on the way home. It has been great knowing I have the support of my son's teachers in helping me raise them. My sons have grown in so many different ways, and the older one has learned so much, from learning about outer space to appropriate table manners."

—**M.B.**

"I have 3 children that have gone and one is currently still going to the same daycare center for almost 13yrs! I needed somewhere for my children to go where people would care for them as much as I do, as they would be spending more waking time there than with me. When I would drop them off in the morning, I was quickly forgotten about, and in the evening when I came to pick them up, I would wait sometimes up to half an hour for them to be ready to leave. The entire time on the way home they would talk about their day and what fun things they did with their teachers and friends. By going to daycare, I feel my kids were better prepared for a classroom setting and already knew how to get along and play with other children. My older children still love to come and visit with their "daycare family" and still talk to their old daycare friends who have grown older and moved away. Having people to grow, laugh, learn and play with…that is a family, and that is what we found in our daycare center."

—**S.S.**

"My son has been going to daycare since he was 6 weeks old! He loves the staff and all the friends he has made through the years. I love that when I come to pick him up, my son has so many stories to tell me about all that happened during the day, what he learned, and the funny things his teachers said. I love it! I love that by him going to daycare it has taught him to speak his mind and be such an outgoing little boy! I feel that once he starts school he will fit in with friends and already know what is to be expected of him in learning and I couldn't thank my daycare enough for teaching him all that!! I can't say enough good things about his daycare and his teachers have done us a great big favor with all they've given him and they have given us the best of memories!"

—**M.V.**

"My experience with both daycare and preschool for my son has been incredible. The excitement on his face and the stories he has about his day warms my heart every time."

—**R.F.**

"I have two children, one who attended daycare when she was younger, and the other who has been attending the same daycare now for two years. I had my daughter in a large chain center and I will never do that again as I felt she was constantly being neglected! Now, with our son in a new daycare, it's a different story. Having him in the right daycare has made him confident, outgoing and more loving then ever! Every staff member in the center knows my child by name and loves him! Everyone there is fabulous! I can ask any question about my child's day and get the answers right away! The teachers are in tune with all the kids and I love it when my son's teacher tells me the funny things my son does or says on any given day. It really shows me that his teachers care and pay attention to him. I was a little nervous at first about trying another center, but after meeting and speaking to the director, who is very hands on in the center, I knew this was the right place for us! My gut told me so and it's the best decision I ever made! I learned that finding the right daycare where you feel comfortable with all the staff is definitely important and can make all the difference in the experience. I love seeing my son learn so much and grow from being a little toddler into a little man." J

—**L.A**

My child has been in daycare since he was three months old, he is now seven. I went to work not feeling guilty for leaving him. I knew he was in good hands! My son has been with his day care provider since the beginning so there's definitely a bond. I don't know what I would've done without a wonderful childcare provider along the way. Let's face it…she sees him more than I do. She has helped mold him into the smart, funny, handsome little boy he is today. She has always made my son feel at home. She has strived to create a home away from home atmosphere for my child and has done an excellent job. She's like a second mother to him. She's constantly flexible to meet our needs. She is responsible, creative and fun. She is equipped with the tools necessary to encourage and inspire the independence that is so important in the physical and cognitive development in children. I am always so impressed by her energy and spirit. I can't say enough good things about her. She will always have a special place in our hearts.

—**SD**

DAY*care*
diaries

*Unlocking the Secrets
and Dispelling the Myths
Through* **TRUE STORIES**
of Daycare Experiences

Rebecca McLaughlin
& Rita Palashewski

NEW YORK

DAY*care* diaries
Unlocking the Secrets and Dispelling the Myths
Through **TRUE STORIES** of Daycare Experiences

Published in New York, New York, by Morgan James Publishing. Morgan James and The Entrepreneurial Publisher are trademarks of Morgan James, LLC. www.MorganJamesPublishing.com

The Morgan James Speakers Group can bring authors to your live event. For more information or to book an event visit The Morgan James Speakers Group at www.TheMorganJamesSpeakersGroup.com.

Disclaimer: The following true stories represent both center and home daycare experiences. The advice given is meant to inform and educate readers, but in no way guarantees that, when utilized, will produce desired results or always keep children safe.

A **free** eBook edition is available with the purchase of this print book.

ISBN 978-1-63047-313-6 paperback
ISBN 978-1-63047-314-3 eBook
ISBN 978-1-63047-315-0 hardcover
Library of Congress Control Number:
2014942384

CLEARLY PRINT YOUR NAME ABOVE IN UPPER CASE

Instructions to claim your free eBook edition:
1. Download the BitLit app for Android or iOS
2. Write your name in **UPPER CASE** on the line
3. Use the BitLit app to submit a photo
4. Download your eBook to any device

Cover Design by:
Rachel Lopez
www.r2cdesign.com

Interior Design by:
Bonnie Bushman
bonnie@caboodlegraphics.com

In an effort to support local communities, raise awareness and funds, Morgan James Publishing donates a percentage of all book sales for the life of each book to Habitat for Humanity Peninsula and Greater Williamsburg.

Get involved today, visit
www.MorganJamesBuilds.com

Habitat
for Humanity®
Peninsula and
Greater Williamsburg
Building Partner

To my mother and my biggest cheerleader, Josephine Missakian, who passed just before the printing of this book. You always sacrificed for your six children and put yourself second, now I want to put you first. Thank you, Mom, for all your love, protection & guidance, and for teaching me by your example what a loving mom is all about, which I can now be for my own children. I love you Mom, more than you'll ever know.

—*Rita*

To my family…

To my husband Shamus: Thank you for your constant love and support through all of my crazy ideas and endeavors…this by far being the craziest!

And to my children, Tyler, Sarah, Stephanie, Neil, Grant, Noel, Rowan, and Molly: Throughout your lives, you have had to make many sacrifices. You have had to share everything from your home to your toys, not to mention your mom, with the many children who came into our home for daycare and became part of the family. Without your generosity and willingness to adapt, this project would never have come to be, and for that I am eternally grateful to each one of you.

I love you all!

—*Becky*

Table of Contents

Introduction

As parents, what do we all want and hope for our children? When they are little, we want them to enjoy their innocence and youth as much as possible and to experience a carefree life for as long as they can. As they grow, we strive to instill in them a strong sense of morals and values while helping them discover their own unique strengths and talents. We hope to fill them with love and security and instill within them a sense of self-love and self-pride that will create a strong foundation and an unwavering confidence to tackle life's challenges. Finally, we attempt to surround them with positive role models with good character and integrity who will assist us in raising them and bringing out their best. We choose and allow others into our children's lives to partner with us and walk alongside us on this journey. Particularly influential will be their early caregivers and teachers, whose hard work and dedication will help us mold and shape our children into the adults they will become.

To these early caregivers, we want to give a voice. We want to acknowledge all the daycare providers who do an outstanding job everyday but go unnoticed, and bring notice to the ones who may be in the wrong field, possibly causing more harm than good. We recognize and commend the providers who give their heart and soul each day in caring for and teaching children. Through this recognition, we hope they realize the magnitude of responsibility they have been given in choosing this field of work. We want daycare providers to consider the safety and well-being of the children they care for as they've never considered before and be more aware of the level of care they are currently providing. We also hope to be that voice that will open parents' eyes to the realities that exist in some daycare settings and help prevent even one more avoidable tragedy from occurring.

From the beginning, we have had a much larger vision for this book than just a career accomplishment or a goal to achieve. Throughout the course of our careers in the childcare business, we have seen the many and repeated obstacles both parents and providers face, and felt education and awareness in these areas were long overdue. With our extensive experience in both home and center daycares, we can clearly see where changes are so desperately needed. We have seen firsthand not only the joy that a quality childcare experience can offer but also the mistakes and misconceptions that are continually made.

We know parents strive to make the best decisions for their children, and many make those decisions based on information provided. Our goal is to provide parents with information that could only be acquired by being on the inside of a childcare center and home daycare for many years. We want to give hope to parents that daycare can be a wonderful experience, but open their eyes to things they would never know or consider, but should know. Our children deserve to be loved, to feel secure and to be cared for by providers that are passionate about working with children. They deserve the best, and it's time for us to step up and make sure that the best is what we are providing them with the choices we make.

We hope the valuable lessons that have been relayed to you through this collection of true stories will allow you to gain new insight, make you laugh as well as cry, and cause you to see things in a whole new light. We hope you walk away with a greater understanding of not only your child but the little world that they spend so much time in…the little world of daycare.

Our ultimate wish for our children is
to grow wings while they are in our care,
so when they leave us, they can fly.

Section I:

The Parents

We all know that being a parent is one of the hardest yet most rewarding jobs in the world. It's a job that does not come with a lot of hands-on training and, to most parents' surprise, their children are not delivered with instructional manuals. It's a role that comes with great responsibility and the weight of that responsibility may seem extremely overwhelming at times.

From the day your baby is born until the day they leave your nest, you will be making many difficult decisions for them and the choices you make can often have a huge impact on the life they choose to lead. Making the decision to place your child in daycare, whether by choice or by necessity, will be one of those difficult decisions. You are essentially deciding to entrust your child's safety and well-being to another... in most cases, a complete stranger. This decision can be very scary and it is not one to be taken lightly or jumped into blindly. Your child's first caregivers will not only be influential but also instrumental in shaping them into the person he or she will become. They will offer your child not only guidance in practical matters, but also help shape their morals, values, self-worth and self-esteem. Thus, it's essential to become well-informed and choose those first care providers wisely.

What's hard to understand is that while parents spend hours educating themselves and reading books on how to raise their children, they know very little about what constitutes a quality childcare program. Many parents will gladly hand their children over to a provider that makes wonderful sounding promises, while not really knowing the person nor whether those promises will actually be fulfilled. These parents will then go to work feeling worried and nervous about their decision, but few of them will know what to do differently.

By sharing our stories and years of experience in the childcare industry, we will open your eyes to the reality that exists behind closed doors in daycare centers and home daycares each and every day. By giving you a glimpse of your child's day from a different perspective, you will suddenly think of questions you never thought to ask, and notice things you never thought to look for. You will also gain a greater appreciation for your child's daycare provider which in turn will create a better daycare experience for you and your child. When it comes to finding the right daycare, knowing how to make educated and informed decisions is where the real journey begins.

 **1.**

The Journey Begins...
Where Do I Start?

Much like the scene in The Wizard of Oz where Dorothy suddenly finds herself in a brightly-colored world custom-made for little people, many parents also find themselves in unfamiliar territory when it comes to the search for the right daycare. Walking into a daycare center or home daycare for the very first time can be a strange experience and many are overwhelmed and unsure of what to expect. Most parents don't have a true understanding of what a quality childcare program should offer so they don't know exactly what to ask or what to look for during their search. What does a quality childcare program really consist of and how much of what you see during a tour is realistically happening each day?

When you have children and you are preparing for the huge transition of placing them in daycare, you are setting out on a journey which can bring about a roller coaster of emotions. You may experience fear, anxiety, excitement and/or guilt all at the same time, and all these emotions are completely normal and to be expected. Even the most planned and prepared parents may experience last minute doubts and fears and occasionally second-guess their choices. Having confidence that you have made the right daycare decision will keep these emotions from getting the best of you and allow you to drop off your child on their first day without completely falling apart. The real question, then, is how can you be sure you are making the right daycare choice for your child?

Becoming educated and knowing what to look for in a quality childcare program will get you headed in the right direction. Knowing you've asked the right questions, received the right answers, and ensured you and your child both feel comfortable in this new environment will alleviate many of your fears and help you both get through those first few rough days with a little more ease. We know how it feels to let go of control and trust someone else to care for your child. In sharing these stories, we hope to help you gain clarity and prepare you for what to expect along the way and offer reassurance that a successful outcome is indeed possible. If you fail to plan, you can plan to fail, but, like Dorothy, if all the right steps are taken down the long winding yellow brick road, daycare can be the beginning of a wonderful journey for both you and your child.

The Insurance Plan

Recently, I met a mom that was just a few weeks away from having her first child. She had a cute little round belly, a beautiful glow on her face and she just about burst with excitement every time she mentioned her baby. I was actually meeting with this woman to discuss insurance needs but, shortly after I walked into her office, the topic quickly turned to daycare.

Upon entering her office, I immediately noticed that her small, tidy space was a bit cramped. She had a portable crib set up in one corner, and a swing, bouncy chair and changing table in another. I assumed that she had probably decided to work while taking care of the baby, but when I asked, she explained that she had actually enrolled her baby at the daycare center right across the street. Now this seemed strange to me, but once again, I assumed that she probably didn't get much of a maternity leave and wanted to have the baby in her office for a short time. Once again, I was wrong. This happy, glowing, soon-to-be new mom looked at me and said, "I'm not sure if I will be able to just sit here and work knowing my baby is across the street being cared for by strangers, so I plan to go get him a lot." I immediately started to laugh as I completely understood and sympathized with this mom. What mom *hasn't* dropped their child off at daycare and then cried all the way to work?

When I explained to her that I had done daycare for years both at home and in a center, I could instantly see that she looked relieved as if she had been thrown a lifeline in her sea of worries and fears. She asked me what she was supposed to do when she missed her baby. How was she supposed to get any work done and what if she cried all day? Having been on the other side of this coin for so long, I'd forgotten how hard it must be for new moms to be separated from their babies. As a provider, I realized I was always concerned with only the baby's first day.

I explained to her that it might be a better idea if she went and spent time rocking and feeding her baby in the infant room at the center, rather than bringing her baby back and forth to work, in between clients. Her eyes opened wide and she looked at me like I was crazy! "Can I really do that?" Now I was the one that was surprised... "It's your baby!" I said, and reassured her that any quality daycare should have an open-door policy for parents. They should welcome you to come at any time, to see, feed, rock, and just bond with your baby. I also stated that by doing this, she would get to know the child's caregivers in a more personal way and begin to develop more trust in them. Her baby would also become used to his new environment sooner if he stayed there all day and got used to a routine. I encouraged her to call the daycare whenever she felt the need to…call to ask how the baby is, what the baby is doing, to express any concerns, or just to say you're missing him. She took comfort in knowing that a quality daycare provider would understand and be happy to hear from her and put her at ease.

By the end of our conversation, she seemed tremendously relieved, repeatedly saying over and over how happy she was to have met me and been given all this new information. She now felt she could move the nursery out of her office and bring it back home, with the exception of the tiny bassinet, and felt empowered and confident that she could be a working mom who wouldn't be crying at her desk all day. I still wondered why her new daycare hadn't reassured her in all of these areas but she did mention that on her tour she really hadn't known what to ask and in the back of her mind she knew she had a back-up office/nursery. I don't think an insurance policy was bought that day but that visit happened for a much greater reason. I walked away wondering how many moms sit at their desks each day missing their babies without knowing what to do about it. As I left the office, she called out to me from down the hall, "Someone should really write a book about all this stuff!" "Thanks," I replied knowingly, "I'll keep that in mind."

Just Around the Corner

When my own search for daycare began (back in the day), I opened up the yellow pages and there it was! Unbeknownst to me, after living in my current home for over a year, there was a daycare center right around the corner and up the street. So excited about its proximity, I couldn't wait to go check it out. Having never stepped foot into a home or daycare center before, I had no idea what to expect. I took my excited little girl and off we went to our scheduled visit and tour of our first daycare center.

As we entered the first set of doors leading into the center, I was impressed to find a second door containing a security system that had to be buzzed to let us in. Once inside, we met with the director, who greeted us warmly, and walked us over to the classroom my daughter would be in. I vividly remember looking around and being amazed and delighted as I took in this little world built just for kids. I marveled at the little tables, sinks, and chairs all around me, and at the cubbies where kids kept their personal items. There were even little cots made for the children to lay and nap on. What impressed me further were the lesson plans on the wall detailing what the kids were learning each day. I wasn't even aware at that time that little two-year-olds could learn so much! Continuing to examine the furniture and toys in the classroom, I noticed a big playhouse in the middle of the room that looked dirty, so I ran my fingers over the side of the house, but nothing came off. Noticing my actions and concern, the director explained to me that the house was wiped clean daily, along with the other toys, but that toys didn't look new for long in a room where they are played with and cleaned so often. Aside from being a little nervous about illness and all of the germs my healthy daughter would now be exposed to, I was excited about this new experience for her and happy she'd have a roomful of children her age to play with.

I signed her up feeling confident about my decision, but after she started, I still cried on my way to work each day for the next two weeks. I would spend a little extra time in her classroom each morning to make drop-off easier, but she would still cry each time I left; I'm not sure who it was harder on, me or her. Sometimes she would latch onto me so tightly I had to ask the teachers for help to pry her off so I could leave. This broke my heart, but what made it easier was that each time I returned to pick her up, she was in no rush to leave. She would excitedly show me the things she did that day and would point out some of her favorite toys and friends.

Eventually, dropping her off became easier for both of us, but things still just didn't feel right to me. I complained more than once about her face being dirty, but didn't see much improvement. At least once a week I would see a new "teacher" in her room and when I would call to check on her, which was daily at first, whoever answered usually sounded annoyed and made me feel like I was being a bother. I didn't appreciate feeling uncomfortable about calling to check on my child whom I'd left in someone else's care that was still like a stranger to me. It soon became a place to just drop her off, leave, then pick her up again and go. I didn't feel a sense of belonging or welcome there and it certainly didn't feel like a home away from home, which is what I was ultimately looking for. I eventually pulled her out, but the realizations I made there led me on a path to build and create the kind of environment I had envisioned for my child... the type of environment I felt most parents were hoping to find.

We all have different priorities and different visions of what the perfect daycare should entail. Ultimately, if you are paying enough attention to the signs and keeping your eyes open, you will know if your daycare is the right place for you and your child. I definitely knew I wanted my child in a center, rather than a home daycare, because I felt a center had more to offer and was a safer option, but I still wanted that feeling of a home-away-from-home. I wanted to feel a sense of belonging there but, looking back, I'm not sure if they even knew my first name. Having to identify myself as someone's mom each time I called didn't feel right, nor did the fact that I never got a full tour of that center – something I'd overlooked back then which became obvious to me once I began giving parents a full tour of my own center.

It was a great first experience that taught me a lot about the daycare world, but even more about myself and what I wanted for my own children. It gave me the determination and drive to create something different, a center with structured learning and expanded opportunities that would also act and feel as a home-away-from-home for parents and their children. My ongoing goal is to build relationships with each family we serve, to act as their extended family, and to have their children feel loved, accepted and celebrated each day for who they are. Children don't choose to be placed in daycare but we have a choice in where to place them. Choose wisely and your children will someday thank you for it!

Check the Check!

 A good home daycare provider expects parents to come to their initial interview with a list of questions to ask. She expects to show you every room in her house and she expects you to bring your whole family to meet her family while interviewing. These are common occurrences at a daycare interview and also a good opportunity for you to see how your child interacts with not only the provider, but with her children and family as well. Each parent handles these situations differently. Many parents come to the initial meeting without their children and arrange a later time for the provider to meet their kids while others bring their children and spend hours just getting to know the provider and letting intuition be their guide. No matter how you choose to find a provider, the bottom line is you need to feel with 100% certainty that you are making the right decision. Make sure you check everything that needs to be checked and there's no doubt left in your mind that your child is in the best possible environment to get the best possible care.

A new mom had called to schedule an interview with a home daycare provider who came highly recommended. She was only six months pregnant, but she was a planner! She wanted every last detail ironed out before she hit the delivery table and she was confident that she would leave no stone unturned to find perfection. She had actually already interviewed several providers that didn't quite make the cut for one reason or another and she was ready to keep looking.

She arrived at her interview, which was at a home very close to her own, with her list of every possible question that could be asked *and* a long checklist of do's and don'ts for the provider. She spent several hours getting to know the potential provider and her family, while checking out every square inch of the house. She had gotten such a great feeling by the end of her visit that she informed the provider she was sure this was the right place for her new baby.

Several months later and a few short days before the baby would start daycare, the mom stopped by with her new little bundle of joy. She stated she was excited to return to work and wanted to make sure she had everything taken care of beforehand. She unpacked clothes, diapers, wipes, a brand new car seat and her neat little stack of paperwork with every "i" dotted and every "t" crossed. What she did next was rather puzzling to the provider. She handed over a check for her child's first week of daycare, but the provider's first name was the only thing written on the "pay to" line. When the provider questioned her about it, she lightly brushed it off and replied that she wasn't sure of her last name and asked the provider to fill in that part. This came as quite a shock to the provider who thought that the mom, upon the initial interview, would have at least had her checked out by the FBI if not a private investigator!

Why would a parent spend so much time getting to know a provider, her family, her home and her schedule, but then solely rely on her instincts or the feeling she got rather then check out the facts? As a parent, it is your job to keep your children safe. If a provider might have something to hide, it is your job to find it. Yes, intuition should play a huge role in your day-to-day relationship with your daycare provider, but if you have one bit of doubt about leaving your children in someone's care, then you shouldn't leave them with that person. Don't walk away without asking that question that's weighing on your mind or go to work if you're feeling doubt about anything at all. Address the issues as they arise and don't ever be afraid to speak up. After all, your child's safety and well-being might just depend on it.

Pop-Ins

Growing up, I remember always having a steady stream of relatives and neighbors popping by unannounced, at any given moment, to visit and have Turkish coffee with my parents. When I first opened my daycare center, it felt like that all over again…

After operating for only a few months, I had many parents that just showed up at my center unannounced wanting a tour. When I would ask parents how they found or heard about us, many would say they were just driving by and decided to "pop in". My staff and I were able to give most parents an "on the spot" tour, but soon, as we became busier, it became harder and harder to accommodate tours that just stopped by. At that point, we realized even though it was still important to maintain an open-door policy so parents could feel free to stop in at any time, if they wanted a proper tour, they would need to make an appointment.

What parents need to keep in mind is that a tour by appointment may not give them a true portrayal of how the room being toured is realistically being run so they should make a point of popping in unannounced before a final decision is made. When a center has a tour scheduled, chances are they will have that room looking and operating at its best for that scheduled time, so it's important to also see it when company is not expected. Every now and then, whether a tour is scheduled or not, a room can fall apart and be a complete disaster and, unfortunately for us, this is how one family experienced it during their tour…

A family that had never used daycare before had set up an appointment to tour our preschool room, and they were quite nervous and excited to meet with us and begin the process of touring daycares. After a brief introduction in the lobby, I walked the parents into the preschool room, where lunch was just getting served. As I was introducing the staff and responding to all the "hellos" from the children, one child's nose started to bleed. This child would have random nose bleeds from time to time, so it was nothing for us to be alarmed about, but definitely something that needed immediate attention. While the teacher tended to the bloody nose, the assistant monitored the other 17 children. Soon, everything went haywire!

As one child spilled the pitcher of milk all over the table, another child, who had just recently moved up from the toddler room, had an accident and began to cry as a "puddle" formed in his seat and under his chair. I apologized to the parents standing there in mid-tour and jumped right in to help. The startled parents watched quietly and waited patiently until once again things were under control. Then I resumed the tour, showing them the entire center and ending with, "It's usually not this crazy." I was pretty sure they didn't believe me and I didn't expect to hear from them again. However, to my surprise, they called us back three days later, after finishing their round of daycare tours, to let my staff and I know they decided to enroll their child at our center. Despite the craziness, they had found what they were looking for in a quality childcare center: staff that knew the children personally and cared more about helping the children than trying to impress and enroll another family. Genuine care, concern, and sincerity will always shine through and rise to the top.

Touring daycares is a very different experience than popping into other kind of facilities for a quick tour. Make sure you have the time needed to observe, ask about, and evaluate everything you see and hear during a tour in order to determine if you feel 100% comfortable with that daycare. An appointment is highly recommended since additional staff may not always be available at any given moment to provide a tour. Keep in mind that a thorough tour could take anywhere from 20 minutes to an hour; my longest tour was close to 2 hours! Once you've completed your tour, ask if you are allowed to return with your child and spend time in your child's classroom, at your convenience. If the center or home daycare provider does not allow this, then think twice about choosing that provider. No center or provider is perfect, but there shouldn't be anything to hide either, so parents should be encouraged to return for additional unannounced visits as they wish.

Ultimately, you will form your own opinion of any daycare that you visit or tour, especially when you see them in action. Go with your gut instinct and when you're on the fence, ask more questions and spend more time there until you feel certain. Always make sure you ask to see every classroom in any center or room in a home daycare, not just the ones your child will be in as well as the outside play area. Being thorough with your search, and popping in at different times to observe mealtime and naptime routines will give you an overall better sense of the experience that awaits your child.

2.

It Never Hurts to Ask...

So why don't we do it more often?

H ave you ever sat in a doctor's office feeling helpless and confused as the doctor impatiently explained something complicated or frightening to you? Then just as you begin processing this new information, the doctor hurries off to his next patient before you get a chance to ask more than a few questions. When you get home, you Google and sort through all this new information only to be flooded with a million more questions that you now want to ask the doctor...but you hesitate. You start thinking about how busy the doctor must be and, after all, you're not his only patient. You should've asked more questions before you left but with all these uncertain facts now flying at you, you really didn't know what else to ask. Soon you have completely talked yourself out of calling the doctor and that is utter craziness! The funny thing is, we sometimes forget the reason doctors have their job in the first place is because of us, the patients. Surely our health is their priority and they are prepared and willing to answer our questions and educate us about our healthcare choices as needed. But when we as patients fail to speak up, call back, or ask the questions that weigh so heavily on our minds, we are only hurting ourselves and preventing the doctors from doing their job to the best of their ability. If they are not aware of the areas where we require guidance and reassurance, then they cannot begin to offer it to us.

This same crazy phenomenon happens in childcare all the time! Many parents go to work each day feeling like they should have asked a question or mentioned a concern, but didn't for one reason or another. Whether a parent is just beginning the daycare journey or has had kids in daycare for years, providers understand that questions and concerns are bound to arise from time to time, and we encourage you to address these issues immediately. Throughout the years, we have heard many parents mention that they didn't call their providers when they had concerns because they didn't want to bother them. Whether it is to check on your child or to simply ask a question, you should never feel like you are bothering your daycare provider, and if you feel like you are, then clearly you have made the wrong choice.

Parents depend on daycare providers to be able to go to work, just as daycare providers depend on having children to care for to be able to work as well. Their job is to help you do the most important job in your life, which is to raise your child. Providers rely on your guidance, your questions and your concerns about your child to help them improve their performance and do their job to the best of their abilities. We are here to discourage you from making false assumptions; instead, pick up your phones and call your providers whenever you feel the need or desire to. This is your child we are talking about, not your cable subscription (which you would actually probably call about)! We want you to ask, question, comment, and inform your providers about anything and everything that crosses your mind at any point, especially when you feel uneasy. When you hesitate to do so, they are often left puzzled, thinking, *How could they have left their child with us without knowing or asking about such-and-such?*

Baby Bottle Blues

A new mom with a four-month-old baby had enrolled her son in a home daycare and was very pleased during his first few weeks there. Her son was always happy and smiling when she came to pick him up and the provider had nothing but kind words to say about her new bundle of joy! Placing her son in daycare had been an extremely

hard thing for her to do and she had looked at many daycares during her search that had honestly scared her. This small home daycare, where a friend also had her child enrolled, had seemed and so far proved to be the perfect choice.

One afternoon, as the mom was picking up her baby, she mentioned to her provider that she would not be going home for several hours as she had errands to run and asked the provider to make her baby a bottle to take along with her. The provider was happy to do so and she quickly grabbed one of the child's bottles from his basket and mixed a bottle of formula for him to go. The mom then thanked her and she and her baby were off on their way to run errands and enjoy the weekend together.

When the following Monday rolled around and the mom returned to daycare with her baby, the provider noticed she seemed quieter than normal and had a feeling something might be bothering her. After several days of feeling like this, the provider finally confronted the mom and asked her if something was wrong. The mom immediately burst into tears and said that yes, something was very wrong, but she wasn't going to say anything because she was afraid of her child losing his daycare. The mom proceeded to tell the provider that she had found mold in the bottle she had been given the week before and was completely horrified that her son had consumed an entire bottle that could have made him very sick! She became enraged as she continued to tell the provider how upset she was and she even pulled out her phone to show the provider pictures that she had taken of the moldy bottle.

The provider stood there completely speechless and embarrassed as she listened to the mom and began to understand just how serious of a mistake she had made. She normally washed the babies' bottles, which had many pieces, and then laid them out to dry. Recently, in trying to be more efficient, she had been putting them back together before they had completely dried and placing them back in the children's baskets. She was sure this was what had caused the mold to grow but regardless of the cause, this mistake should never have happened. She apologized to the mom and refunded her for several days of care. She also bought the baby all new bottles and promised to send them home each night to be inspected by his mom. In the end, his mom decided to keep her child in that daycare and give the provider another chance. After all, everyone makes mistakes, right?

You may be wondering why this mom waited an entire week to speak up about something she was so clearly distraught over. She continued to bring her son for several more days, even though she feared he could be fed from more bottles that could contain mold, without saying a word! A good daycare provider will always take responsibility for their actions. Mistakes, sometimes even big ones, can and will happen. At the same time, providers rely on parents to speak up when something is wrong, bring issues immediately to their attention and question things that just don't seem right. Providers cannot begin to remedy situations they are completely unaware of. There should never be fear or hesitation to speak up when your child is concerned. Your child is relying on you to be their voice and your provider is relying on your voice to help them do their job to your satisfaction.

Time to Vent!

One day, a parent whose profession it was to clean office buildings was disturbed by a sight she saw while dropping her son off in his classroom at daycare. The vent that circulated fresh air into the room looked overly dusty and badly overdue for a cleaning. Being in the cleaning business, this bothered her more than it probably did most parents, who may or may not have even noticed it. This issue continued to bother her, day in and day out, for over a week and she was becoming frustrated that nothing was being done about it. One morning she finally decided to bring this issue to the director's attention.

She first asked the director if the center might be in need of some extra outside cleaning services. When she was politely told no, she then finally mentioned the vent. She nervously stated that although this issue bothered her very much, she had been very happy with everything else in her child's classroom and with his care, so she didn't want to create any negative feelings by bringing it up. This was shocking to the director for many reasons and she explained to the parent that they did indeed have a cleaning checklist. This item must have been missed or neglected by the cleaning staff, and the director assured her that it would be taken care of immediately. The director then thanked the parent for bringing it to her attention, and she urged the parent to never again hesitate to bring up an issue or concern of any kind. The parent felt instantly relieved for bringing it up and realized how silly it had been to not have brought it up sooner.

This is a common occurrence in daycare settings. Whether the issue is cleanliness or a child's behavior, parents are reluctant to speak up. By speaking up, you will accomplish two very important things. First, you will determine if the things that are important to you are also important to your provider. Second, you will be able to determine by the action taken after you have raised an issue, if the provider is the right provider for your child. Your issues should always be addressed in a timely manner with a resolution that you feel is acceptable to you and your child. The best advice that we can give to a parent is to never walk away from your child's daycare feeling like you should have said something, and didn't. You just never know when your words will make a difference in the life of a child, be it your own or another's.

• • • • •

One day while playing at the park with my daycare kids, I noticed a large van pulling into the parking lot, which was a good distance away from the playground. A minute later, several children came running over to the playground, followed by their daycare provider, and began playing. The provider had seven children in her group and after playing for about 20 minutes, I watched her leave the kids and walk over to her van. As she opened the side doors, I could clearly see two rear facing infant car seats in the first row. A few seconds later, she closed the doors and returned to the park to join her group. She checked on the van one more time another 20 minutes later. I was quite curious about this behavior so as I was leaving with my daycare kids, I walked by her van and sure enough, I found 2 infants sleeping in their car seats, all alone.

• • • • •

Beware of the Stairs...

A mom had enrolled her 10-month-old baby in a home daycare and she had been very happy with her decision. After months of questioning providers and thoroughly examining their homes, she felt confident that the right choice had been made. This provider had been caring for children for many years, and had several children of her own. Only one thing bothered her, and that was the steep set of stairs leading into the downstairs playroom which she noticed were never gated. Now, after several months had passed, her baby was more mobile and this became an even greater concern. Although she was fearful of her daughter's safety, she was also reluctant to bring this up, worried that she might offend her provider by implying she was incompetent.

Meanwhile, whenever she would come to pick up her baby, she would ask the other children how their day went, and on one particular day she got an earful! It turned out that one of the provider's little girls had fallen down the stairs that morning. Upon hearing this, the mom was shocked and her worst fears were confirmed. Before she could even process her thoughts, her daycare provider quickly stepped in to fill her in on the details of what had actually occurred.

The provider's seven-year-old daughter had a hooded sweatshirt on that morning, and thought it would be funny if she wore it backwards to cover her face. Well, she did exactly that, and while the provider was preparing her children's lunches for school, her daughter had walked around blindly toward the steps and had fallen down. The provider assured the mom that her own daughter was fine and explained that she was very diligent in watching those stairs where the younger daycare children were concerned. (As most of us know, you needn't be worried about a seven-year-old falling down steps…unless of course, they have their eyes covered!)

The image of her own baby falling down those stairs was now playing in the mom's head, and she finally felt that it was a perfect opportunity to express her growing concern. She explained to the provider that she had been worried for months about those steep stairs, and couldn't understand why a gate was not securing them. The provider was taken aback at first and then asked the mom why she had never said anything about this before, especially since she had been so thorough with everything else. The mom was now embarrassed and explained to her that she trusted her completely and hadn't wanted to question her judgment. The provider appreciated her trust, but told her she shouldn't ever worry about offending someone else at the expense of her child's safety. She continued to explain that she had tried using a gate in the past, but it seemed to attract more children to it. She feared if pushed upon, the gate could snap, causing a child to fall. She reassured the mom that whenever her child was playing in that area, she would push 2 couches together to create a space that her child couldn't get through to reach the stairs.

It doesn't make sense that a parent would worry more about offending someone's feelings than putting their child's safety first. It's understandable that most people don't want to cause a stir, but this is not acceptable when it comes to your child. Create all the stir that's necessary to keep your child safe! It made the mom feel better to hear all the precautions the provider was taking to protect her child, and she felt bad that it had taken an accident to realize how important it was to just speak up whenever she had concerns. This is your child we are talking about and if you don't speak up, who will? It never hurts to ask…but it may end up hurting your child not to.

Don't Feel Bad

Many times parents are reluctant to bring up a concern or make a complaint about a teacher because they "feel bad" and "don't want to get them in trouble". One mom went so far as to say she felt like a "nark" for tattling on her child's teacher. Parents need to understand that their concerns should be considered a top priority at daycare. Teachers are often not even aware that something they did (or didn't do) was taken offense to if it's not brought to their attention. Most teachers that take pride in the care they offer will appreciate the feedback and use it to improve their performance.

On two separate occasions, a mom picked up her son from daycare with wet pants. Both times when she arrived, the children were laying down watching a movie. She realized the teacher may not have noticed these accidents, given the situation, but she was still bothered by it and felt that the children should have been monitored more closely. She was also concerned about the amount of T.V. time the children were having and questioned the movie choices the teacher allowed. After the second occurrence, still hesitant, she finally brought her concerns to the director's attention.

The first thing the director asked was if these concerns had been brought to the teacher's attention yet. The mom replied, "no" because she felt uncomfortable in doing so, and didn't want the teacher to be intimidated by her or treat her child differently because she was complaining. Also, this teacher was fairly new and the mom hadn't felt like she had really bonded with her yet. The director understood her situation and encouraged her to take the time to get to know staff so she would feel more comfortable to discuss issues that came up. She also reminded her that a good team takes everyone's participation, and her child's teachers, as well as the director, were on that team with her, where open and honest communication were key to a successful outcome. If the mom felt at any point her concerns were not being addressed by the teachers to her satisfaction, then she should come to the director.

The following day, these concerns were addressed with the teacher, and later the director shared the conversation with the mom. Unfortunately, a misunderstanding about the center's T.V. rules and the teacher forgetting which children needed extra potty reminders, were the cause for the undesirable incidents that had occurred. As the mom listened, she understood how busy childcare teachers could be and appreciated the immediate attention taken to resolve these issues. She also didn't have any bad feelings toward the teacher and realized she should've spoken up sooner (to her child's teacher) before the problems occurred a second time. She promised going forward, she would keep open lines of communication with her child's teachers and work with them on issues as they arose.

In this example, it's a child whose clothes didn't get changed, but this story rings true for so many issues parents neglect to bring up to avoid hurting the teacher's feelings. We understand the sensitivity aspect of complaining to or about someone you and your child will still be interacting and working closely with daily. At the same time, this is precisely the reason why it is so important to bring these issues up immediately. We want to impress upon you the importance of being your child's voice and advocate in their daycare and in their life! Things will get missed and problems will occur; the important factor is, once an issue is brought up, is immediate action taken toward resolving it? The right provider will always make you feel glad you came forward and will offer you a solution that should bring you peace of mind.

3.

When to Wonder,
When to Worry...
What do you think really happened here?

W e've probably all been guilty at one time or another of jumping to false conclusions or placing blame before we actually knew all the facts surrounding a situation. One day, two of my daughters were rolling around on the floor and playing together, when suddenly my younger daughter burst into tears. She was holding her leg and crying out hysterically in pain! Now, any mom knows that we all have what's called "the mama bear" that

 lives inside of us, and when our children get hurt or mistreated, that mama bear comes out, ready to attack anything or anyone in her way! I immediately lost my temper and accused my older daughter of kicking her sister and without letting her explain, I sent her to her room, enraged that she would do such a thing! Well, a few minutes later, I discovered that my younger

20

daughter had actually hurt her leg by rolling over onto a block while playing. I felt horrible about falsely accusing my older daughter, and immediately went over to her and apologized for my actions. When a child gets hurt or mistreated, it's natural to look for someone else to blame, and when an accident happens at daycare, a parent's first response is to blame the provider.

Unfortunately accidents and incidents can happen anywhere, including daycare. In addition, daycares are very busy places with a lot going on at any given moment, which would naturally increase the chances of mishaps occurring. It's not fair to assume that whenever a mishap or accident occurs involving a child at daycare, it must be due to the lack of supervision, carelessness, or negligence on the provider's part. It's important for parents to see the whole picture and get all the details of an incident before making assumptions about the level of care that was being provided when the incident occurred. Once a parent has all the information, they can determine whether they truly need to worry about the care their child is receiving or just accept all the natural craziness that can occur in such a setting...

Finger-Painting Without Paint

It's naptime in the Toddler Room...the lights are off, the curtains are drawn and lullabies are softly playing in the classroom. After a busy morning, and a satisfying lunch, all the toddlers are sound asleep on their little cots. Some are lying sideways, cuddled with their blankets, while others are lying on their backs with their hands crossed behind their heads as if they are tanning under the sun. It's an  exceptionally adorable sight to see a roomful of little ones sleeping so soundly.

While the children sleep, the teacher has many duties she is responsible for. One afternoon after tending to various cleaning tasks, a teacher had just sat down to begin filling out daily reports when something caught the corner of her eye. She noticed that one little girl had woken up and was lying there quietly, looking up at the ceiling and at all the things around her. The teacher decided to let her be, since she wasn't disrupting nap time.

About 15 minutes later, to the teacher's surprise, the child was still lying quietly on her cot content as can be. Since toddlers are usually the group of kids with the most energy, they almost never sit still or do any one thing for more than ten minutes! This really piqued the teacher's curiosity, and she wondered if the little girl was just extra tired today and maybe needed a little extra rest. From where she sat, she could see that the child was now playing with her fingers and waving her arms around a bit. She decided she would go ask her if she wanted to get up and do some quiet activities until the others awoke.

As she began walking toward the child, the pungent aroma of a freshly filled diaper hit her nose like a brick wall and she realized a major diaper change would be in order! Then, just before she reached her, she noticed the little girl wiggling around on the cot while rubbing her hands between herself and the carpet. Suddenly she discovered why this little girl remained occupied on her cot for so long! She had been busy spreading the contents of her diaper all across her cot and the carpet! At this point, the smell was so overpowering, the teacher could hardly breathe! Oh, what a sight!! She immediately called for extra help and, while the assistant monitored the sleeping children, the toddler teacher focused on cleaning up the little girl and sanitizing the smelly crime scene she had so quietly finger painted!

The fact that this disaster occurred would naturally make one assume that the child was not being watched, which clearly was not the case. The teacher made the decision to leave the child on her cot, which made sense since the child didn't get up on her own. What she should have done differently was to position herself a little closer to the child to make sure she could monitor her more effectively. It isn't uncommon for toddlers to be curious about their diaper contents and this story reminds us all that when a toddler seems a little too quiet, be weary! It's important for parents to remember that incidents like this can happen at home as well. Depending on the incident, it may be reasonable to let it go once, but recurring incidents should clearly be a sign to wonder less and worry more!

• • • • •

One day, in my own home daycare, I assumed that all the kids in my care were napping so I took the opportunity to start dinner for my family. Being in the kitchen, I was not in direct sight or sound of all the children. After about 20 minutes, I decided to check on the two three-year-old boys that I thought were napping soundly.

I was horrified to discover that they instead were colorfully decorating my brand new couch with markers! Needless to say, I learned my lesson and began carrying a baby monitor around the house like a teenager carries a cell phone!

• • • • •

Guess Who I Ran Into?

Many times in home daycares, providers will take the kids they are caring for along with them to run personal errands to just about any place they need to go. Some parents are fine with this and actually welcome the fact that their kids will be getting out of the house more often. Other parents are okay with their children going on kid-friendly outings only, like to the park or library, and then there are the parents who don't want their kids transported at all. These outings or field trips usually don't present a problem as long as parents have an understanding with their providers about the trips their kids will take and when they will occur. It's when parents find out, completely by surprise, that their child has been taken somewhere unbeknownst to them, that a good daycare situation can go very quickly downhill.

One day a home daycare provider took her group of 7 children to a large grocery store to get supplies for a baking project for the kids to do, as well as some other items she needed. She had been taking her daycare kids to the store, the post office and wherever else she needed to go, for years and had rarely mentioned these outings to parents at the end of the day. It was just part of her day and she felt parents chose home daycares knowing that kids would be treated like members of the provider's family; therefore, taking them along to run personal errands seemed perfectly acceptable.

When she arrived at the store, she placed the baby in the front of the cart and the 2 smaller children in the back. The rest of the kids wandered behind her like little baby ducks, as she walked up and down each isle choosing her items. As she pushed her very full cart towards the checkout lanes, she suddenly heard a loud gasp and then a woman's voice saying, "What in the world are you doing here!?" It was the mom of one of the children in her group, looking extremely irritated to find her daughter in the back of a shopping cart, under a heap of groceries, when she was supposed to be in daycare. Not only was this mom surprised that her child was not in daycare, but she was also shocked to discover that her daughter was being taken to public places without her knowledge! Her provider explained very calmly that she always took the kids to run errands and assumed all the parents were aware of this. If parents ever asked her about outings, she would have let them know, but they rarely asked. She also pointed out that in her daycare contract, which every parent signed, it clearly stated that the provider would occasionally be transporting her daycare kids as needed. She had been doing this for years, and until now, this matter had never been an issue with any of the other families.

The mom was completely stunned to learn this fact and couldn't comprehend how this had been happening for so long without her ever knowing it. A million questions were now racing through her mind, such as, *Where else has my child been and how safe is it to actually have this many kids with one person in a public place?* By discovering this one fact by accident, she now doubted the safety and the quality of the daycare she had loved just that morning when she had dropped off her daughter. She had originally chosen this provider because she offered Saturday care and was conveniently located and, over the past two years, she'd been really happy with her choice. It had never even occurred to her to ask questions about her child being taken to the grocery store! Weren't kids supposed to go to daycare to just play and learn?

The reassurance of knowing where your child is at all times and that they are safe is one of the most important things a daycare should offer. After this incident occurred, the parents of this child removed her from this daycare and ended up placing her in a family member's home which, while less convenient, made them feel safer. Unfortunately, when trust is broken between a parent and a provider, it can almost never be regained. We all love convenience, but when it comes to quality childcare, convenience should be at the bottom of the list, and asking important questions and knowing pertinent facts about providers and their practices should come first. Read your daycare provider's contract thoroughly and make sure you are clear and agree to all the terms before signing.

An Unpleasant Surprise

When my first child started daycare as a toddler, she was just starting to potty train and wear underwear. She was doing well overall, and would have a few accidents here and there, but typically not while she was at daycare. One day, when I picked her up, I was told she had an accident and her underwear was bagged up and stored in her cubby for me to take home. I wondered why she still had the same clothes on, and just the underwear was bagged...I soon discovered why.

When we got home, I went to the laundry sink and prepared to prewash her underwear before adding it to the rest of the laundry. When I opened up the bag, I wasn't prepared for what I found! A huge piece of poop was sitting in her underwear staring back at me! I jumped in surprise and it rolled and almost fell out onto the floor! No wonder the bag felt fuller than it should've been. When I saw this, I was, to say the least, disgusted, and couldn't understand why the teachers would do such a thing! I was so furious that before doing anything else, I charged toward the phone (after washing my hands of course) to call the center's director.

After the director quietly listened to me as I expressed my concern and frustration over the situation, she calmly explained the procedure for handling potty accidents. In the cases where children soil their underwear, staff are to dump any loose particles from the garment, then wrap it up tightly into a bag to be sent home, but they are not allowed to wash anything out. Once I received a full explanation, the procedure made sense, but in this particular case, that procedure clearly was not followed, resulting in the big surprise waiting for me!

At times, certain events may seem unreasonable until you get the full explanation. It's easy to forget that not all situations can or will be handled at daycare the way you would handle them at home. Even though we trust our providers enough to turn our children's care over to them, as soon as something goes wrong, it's funny how quickly we can turn around and assume the worst! It's important to get all the facts before making any assumptions so as to more accurately determine whether each situation needs more worrying or just more wondering.

Haircut Day

One morning, in a busy home daycare, the provider had set out Play-Doh and cookie cutters and was working with a group of kids around the table. Several of the older kids

began to get bored and wanted to be done. Since the provider needed to clean up the table and get the smaller kids cleaned up as well, she asked the older kids to go upstairs and read books until she was done.

After about 15 minutes, she called the older kids to come down and put their shoes on to go outside. As they wandered down the stairs, one by one, she noticed how quiet they were and immediately suspected that something must be up! One of the boys in the group came down last and she suddenly noticed his hair…or the lack of it. He had big bald patches on the top of his head and his bangs were completely gone! She was speechless at first, then questioned them to find out what had happened. One of the little girls had found scissors in her daughter's bedroom and decided to play barber shop. After cutting several strands of her own long hair, the little girl then decided to give the little boy a haircut too.

The provider realized what poor judgment she had used in letting the older kids play unattended upstairs. She knew she'd have to call the boy's mom to explain the situation and expected his mom to be very upset. Luckily, the little girl's dad was a barber, and worked out of his home which happened to be next door. During their conversation, the boy's mom agreed to let the barber try to fix her son's hair.

The provider nervously walked the whole group next door and anxiously waited outside while the neighbor took the little boy in for a "trim". What a shock it was when they came out a few minutes later and the child was smiling and completely bald! The provider dreaded the moment when his mom would see his new haircut but much to the provider's surprise, his mom laughed when she saw him and said, "What a great look for summer." After this incident, the daycare provider no longer let the older and younger kids separate into groups; she'd use the older kids as "helpers" for the younger children, which helped them get cleaned up and outside much faster.

Home daycare providers are faced with an extremely challenging task when trying to entertain and be fully present with many children of different ages all at the same time. Ask your home daycare provider what she does to keep the older children busy while she is tending to the younger ones. Does she allow the older pre-school aged children to play unsupervised either outside or in a different room? Does she go outside with the older children while the younger ones are napping unattended inside or does she keep her group together and use the older ones to teach the younger ones? Every home daycare provider will have her own way of doing things, but the most important thing to consider is constant supervision. Accidents can occur so quickly, but not all will be as easy to fix as a bad haircut.

 **4.**

Shocking Realities ...
The Ugly Truth of It All

T he whole nation was shocked and enraged when they heard about the mom in Florida who forgot her child in the back seat of her car and went into work. Sadly, the child died of heat exhaustion and everyone assumed that this mother must be a monster! No one could comprehend how a mother could possibly forget about her own child, but after the mother appeared on the Oprah Winfrey show, many hearts and minds were changed.

 This mother described an incident that left many feeling like this tragedy could have easily happened to any one of them. She described a very hectic morning that any busy parent could relate to, where multiple things were happening at once, and many responsibilities were being handled simultaneously. On that particular morning, there was a "break in routine" which caused her to forget that her daughter was still in the car.

The mom worked as an assistant principal at a school, and it was the first day back to work after summer's end. The dad, who usually took their toddler to the babysitter's on his way to work, had a dentist appointment that morning, so he asked the mom to take her instead. The mom loaded her toddler into the car, but realizing it was too early to drop her off, she decided to go pick up donuts for the teachers as a welcome back surprise. As her toddler fell asleep in the back seat, and the mother's head was full of all the things she had to do that morning, she simply forgot she had her daughter with her, and drove straight to work. She did not realize her fatal mistake until 8 hours had passed and it was too late.

As busy parents with so much on our minds, we sometimes run like coffee-powered machines on auto pilot, not fully engaged in what we are actually doing in the present moment. Have you ever driven to work and upon arrival not remembered the ride there at all?

A child can be forgotten just as easily as a childcare provider can lose track of the number of children in her care. When many children are gathered in one place, with so much going on, crazy and scary things are sometimes bound to happen. Some of the choices providers make will not always be in the best interest of the child, which may unintentionally place them in harm's way. Reasons can be as simple as the provider not following policy, not thinking things through, or not being fully engaged in the present moment with the children. Parents can't guarantee their children's safety 100% of the time and unfortunately neither can a provider. We can all just strive to give our very best each and every day. Accidents and undesirable incidents can occur from time to time, but knowing the details that led up to the events will help shed a different light on the situation. Providers should be given fair consideration and understanding by parents when something goes wrong while caring for a child.

• • • • •

Once I forgot my 4th baby, when he was just a few weeks old, at a Chinese restaurant after having lunch with my parents. As soon as I exited the restaurant, I realized that something was missing and I should've been carrying more than just a diaper bag.

• • • • •

Field Trip for One

It was a beautiful summer morning when a Toddler teacher was preparing to take her group of 7 toddlers out to the playground, as she had done many times before. As she gathered her clipboard and other items needed for outside, she opened their classroom door and led them outside to a fenced in area. To the right, about 20 feet away, was the gate leading to their playground, and to the left, about the same distance away, were 2 gates leading to the building's front parking lot. The teacher led her group of two-year-olds toward the right, and as they all walked into the playground after her, she locked the gate behind them.

About 10 minutes later, a parent pulled into the parking lot, only to find a child standing there alone on the curb, in front of the building. Confused, this parent picked up the child and entered the daycare. She approached the director with the child and it was at that moment the director horrifically discovered that this toddler must have gone missing without the teacher realizing it. She was in disbelief that this could've happened. As she thanked the parent, she quickly took the child into her arms and checked him to make sure he wasn't harmed. The child seemed fine, and the director was so relieved yet very shaken up!

After calling the parents to alert them of the situation, she carried the child out to the playground to join his group, and was curious to see his teacher's reaction upon seeing him. How could she *still* have not realized this child was missing? When she arrived at the playground, the teacher saw the child and looked so puzzled...then her puzzled look turned to sheer terror! She realized what had taken place and quickly understood that not only had she lost a child, but she had also been unaware he had been missing for over 15 minutes!

The first mistake that occurred was instead of directing her group from behind and following them into the playground, she led them from the front which didn't allow her to see the child that went the other direction. Second, as the children entered the playground, she should have counted each of their heads to ensure she had all children accounted for before locking the gate behind them. Lastly, even though she didn't do the headcount as kids walked through the gate, she should've done it within a few minutes of being on the playground with them. She had failed to follow these policies, and got into the habit of doing things her own way. Although she was a very loved and appreciated teacher, she was let go immediately, and this mistake ended her career in childcare.

Over time, we can tend to become over confident and neglect the important details and practices that were put into place to keep children safe. Sometimes it can be the smallest step which, when left out, can lead to the biggest disaster. Policies are put into place to ensure a child's safety, but can only be effective when religiously followed. Be sure to inquire about your center's policy regarding headcounts and how often they are done. Also, ask about the procedures for moving kids from place to place, and then take it upon yourself to check if they are being followed. These are not questions a director will hear often, if ever, from parents. Sometimes in asking these questions, it also reminds a director to follow up on policies that may need reinforcing. This situation could have ended tragically if the child had stepped down from the curb and headed toward the street, but luckily he was found in time. When a childcare provider makes a mistake, uses poor judgment or disregards a policy, the cost can be a life, and even the ones with the best intentions cannot afford to take such chances.

Big Scare Under the Big Top

One day early in my daycare career, before I really knew any better, I thought it would be a great idea to take my daycare kids to the circus. I asked all my daycare parents for permission and they all agreed without a second of hesitation. The kids were beyond excited! When the big day arrived, I packed a picnic lunch, a bag of diapers and wipes, emergency contact forms, and off we went to the circus!

The first eye-opening moment occurred for me when we had to park in a parking garage which was quite far away from the actual circus. I had six children with me and one stroller. I formed a line of kids behind the stroller and somehow we all managed to make it to the circus without any major issues. We found our seats quickly and had been seated for about a minute when the first child needed to go to the bathroom. I should have seen this coming, but still quite optimistic about this adventure, I again formed my line and took all the kids to the bathroom, which was very far from our seats. We made it back to our seats right before the show started and the kids sat eagerly as they watched the clowns begin to perform. About five minutes later, a clown was shot from a very loud cannon and a few of them were startled and started to scream and cry. I walked the few kids that were screaming away from the group to try and calm them down and when we returned a few minutes later one of the little three-year-old boys had wandered off. My heart sank and I felt panicked and overwhelmed as I second guessed my decision to ever bring so many small children into such a crowded and chaotic place. Within a few seconds of frantic searching, I spotted the little boy a few rows up in the bleachers and breathed a big sigh of relief. A very nice woman noticed my despair and helped me to gather the kids together and get back outside. I had never been so happy to be safely back in my van with the six kids buckled into their car seats and on the way home.

That was my first and last experience with taking many young children to a busy and over-crowded place. It's just not safe for one person to be taking many children anywhere and as a parent, I would think twice about letting your children go on field trips to busy places without the proper number of adults attending. Many providers that take these fun trips make sure to bring helpers along so the children can be easily managed and scary situations are less likely to occur.

Being a daycare provider is one of the busiest jobs there is and the price for making even the tiniest of mistakes can be extremely high and always comes at the expense of the child. Ask your daycare provider what the policy is for field trips and outings. Will there be more than one adult accompanying the children or will your provider be using a helper and who would that helper be? Also, consider the details of the outing, and do they make sense and seem safe to you? These questions may seem out of the ordinary but having the peace of mind and knowing that your child is safe at all times makes them worth asking.

● ● ● ● ●

When my first child was 5 days old, I decided her first outing would be to my husband's workplace to show her off. I buckled her into her car seat, grabbed my "regular" purse, popped the car seat into the base in the car, and off we went! When we arrived, I took her out of her car seat and carried her in. Ten minutes into showing her off, I had to go to the bathroom, badly! With everyone busy at work, I ran into the bathroom with her in my arms. That's when I realized I didn't know what to do with her while I tended to business. Panicky and about to pee in my pants, I quickly laid paper towels down on the counter by the sink, then laid her on top of them. I was so terrified she may fall, (not realizing that a five-day old baby doesn't move). I felt like a horrible mom and that was my first lesson in making sure I'm fully prepared before ever leaving the house with the baby again!

• • • • •

In a Split Second

At the end of the day, with only a few toddlers left, a toddler teacher brought out some puzzles and asked the kids to gather at the table. Excitedly, they all rushed over and sat down on their little chairs, ready to play! A little boy stood up on his chair, as toddlers often do, and as he tried to jump back down, his body twisted, causing him to fall towards the sink that was nearby. It happened so quickly that the teacher sitting at the table could do nothing to save his fall.

All of a sudden, terrible screams were coming from the small boy and his face was full of blood! The teacher immediately called for help as she grabbed a cloth and applied pressure to the open wound she could clearly see on the child's cheek. The child was hysterical and it took two staff members to calm him down. Meanwhile, his parents had been called and were on their way. The teacher was sick to her stomach and tried her best to remain calm as she took care of him. No one could believe how quickly this quiet activity turned into such a horrendous scene!

When his parents arrived shortly after, the child had begun to calm down and was sitting in his teacher's lap, looking at books. It's amazing how resilient children can be, given the severity of the wound. His parents took him to the emergency room and the next day they contacted the center with an update on his situation. The little boy's cheek had a deep laceration from his cheekbone almost to the corner of his mouth; he received many stitches that could possibly end up leaving him with a scar. They were going to keep him home for the next two days, and planned on bringing him back after that.

Immediately after this incident, the child's teacher, along with the center director, analyzed the cabinet in the toddler room to determine what had taken place. Apparently, a board that couldn't be seen had come loose and the force of the child's fall had caused it to pop out of place and slice into his cheek. They taped up the loose board to make the sink temporarily functional, and a week later it was fully replaced.

This little boy had been attending this daycare center since he was an infant and the parents were very happy with the care their child had been receiving. They had a trusting relationship with both management and staff, and visited the following day to get a detailed account of the events that had taken place. The parents did not feel that negligence was involved, and had no reservations about bringing their child back to the center a few days later. The parents were very understanding about this accident, but it was the staff that suffered each time they saw the child's face, reminding them of an accident they hadn't been able to prevent. As years went by, the wound healed nicely, leaving only the faintest trace of a scar where the cut had been. The family continued their relationship with this daycare, and a decade later, they ended up bringing their second child there as well.

Accidents of varying levels will occur from time to time with some being more extreme than others. What matters most is getting all the information and seeing the full picture when determining if negligence might have been involved. This family had an enormous amount of faith in their daycare center, and they never doubted their good intentions. Still, they did the right thing by following up with staff to get the full story. It's imperative to build a relationship where you feel you can completely rely on and trust your child's provider and the care they offer. After a period of time, if you don't feel that way, then it's time to question and reconsider your choice.

Daily Sheet Disaster

I was working as a teacher in a busy infant room many years ago that enrolled 16 babies under the age of 16 months. We had 4 primary caregivers and each of us was responsible for the care of the same four babies each day. We took care of all of our babies' needs including changings, feedings and naps, and we recorded all the information on daily sheets which parents received at the end of each day. Due to the busy and chaotic nature of the room, daily sheets would often get neglected until the provider had a break, by which time important information would sometimes be forgotten and not recorded. This often would lead to mistakes such as some babies missing diaper changes while others receiving bottles they weren't scheduled to have. Another problem with not filling in daily sheets throughout the day was that when other staff members came in to give the primary teachers a break, they would rely on these daily sheets for information concerning the babies. If they were not properly updated, then mistakes would often occur.

On one particularly busy day, we had a substitute in for one of the primary teachers and several other unfamiliar staff members coming and going to give breaks to the infant staff. Several of the babies were teething and not feeling well and since they required extra attention, the daily sheets along with other responsibilities were getting neglected. By the end of that day, we were just glad to send each baby home safe and sound.

The next morning, one of the parents came in and was furious! It turns out, in all the chaos that had ensued the previous day, we had made a terrible mistake by recording inaccurate information on her child's daily sheet. The result of this negligence was her child going an entire day without a diaper change. Her baby had gone home soaking wet and now had a painful diaper rash. She was shaking with rage as she confronted us and we were actually very afraid for our safety! We certainly couldn't blame her for feeling this way, and we knew no amount of explanations or apologies could fix this situation. The mom never brought her child back to this daycare again and we all felt so horrible that this had taken place.

Even though this mom had been very happy for several months at this daycare and even though we only had the best of intentions, a terrible mistake occurred. When many babies are being cared for in one large room, even when staffed appropriately, mishaps and oversights are more likely to occur. Large daycare centers may offer many advantages, but individual attention and attention to detail that parents expect, can be compromised as rooms fill to capacity. Often, mistakes that providers make are unintentional, but these mistakes can be harmful to the babies and inexcusable to the parents.

5.

Daycares Don't Have Drive-Thrus…

Please Don't Leave Your Orders at the Door!

T hese days everyone seems to be on the fast track to convenience. Everything can be done with the push of a button or minimal effort and people are becoming very accustomed to modern technology and the convenience it allows them. You can deposit your check and order your groceries all from your phone, then go to the grocery drive-thru to pick up your order without ever leaving the comfort of your car. Even our cars are a place of convenience with their built-in navigation systems, dual DVD players and heated steering wheels and seats. We can pay bills in our bathrobes, shop for swimwear in our sweats,

and many people can now work from home without ever being inconvenienced by having to get dressed. Life has become, in many ways, too easy, and many times we see the result of this madness creeping into daycare settings where it really doesn't belong.

It's great when a quality home daycare or center offers you some conveniences like hours to accommodate your schedule or proximity to your work. The problem occurs when parents become a little too accustomed to modern convenience and begin to treat daycare like a one-stop convenience store or a drive-thru where their kids can be ordered to go. If daycares did have drive-thrus, some parents would probably pull up, name the child they wanted delivered, and collect them through the checkout window, without even giving it a second thought.

We want parents to slow down and spend the time with their children that they deserve. Of course there will always be those days when parents are racing against the clock, and need to run in and out as fast as possible, but this shouldn't be a regular occurrence. Make the same time for your kids as you would for other important priorities and commitments in your life. Childcare is not meant to just accommodate the working parent, it is also meant to benefit the child while the parent is at work. Pay enough attention to what they need at daycare to make their experience successful, so you can confidently focus your attention elsewhere while you're away.

Honk Honk!!!

Daycare centers and home daycares are always busy places but can be especially busy at pickup and dropoff times. Parents are coming and going, kids are preparing to either start their day or leave, and providers have many responsibilities associated with opening and closing their classrooms. Parents and providers need to work together during these transitional times so that all runs smoothly and each day can start and end in success.

At the end of a busy day in a small home daycare, the kids were sitting at a table enjoying coloring activities and books as parents were streaming in and out picking up their children. From where the children were sitting, they could see the front driveway of the house through a large window in the living room. They would get really excited whenever they saw their own familiar cars pull up and would run to get their coats and wait by the door for their parents to come in.

The provider was busy briefly chatting with each parent about their child's day and doing last-minute cleaning duties before closing. Meanwhile, a little three-year-old boy recognized his mom's blue van and screamed with excitement as he quickly put his book away and ran to get his things. The provider knew better though and tried to distract him since she knew this child's mom had a habit of sitting in the driveway for long periods of time on her cell phone before coming in. In the past, there were times when the daycare had actually closed and the provider had walked the child to his mom's car. On those occasions, she would watch disappointedly as the boy would climb into his car seat and buckle himself in, with little or no acknowledgment from his mom as she continued her "important" conversation without disruption.

Once the boy's mom pulled into the driveway, she once again remained in the car. This time, the boy finally questioned his provider about why his mom always took so long to come in. After several more attempts to distract the child, the provider decided to address the problem rather than ignore it. She took the little boy by the hand, grabbed his backpack and opened her door leading out to the driveway where they could clearly see Mom busily chatting away in her car. As they stood right outside the front door, the little boy started to jump up and down and wave frantically to get his moms attention to no avail. The provider also motioned for his mom to end her conversation and come to see her child who was so eagerly waiting for her. After a few minutes, his mom ended her call and hurried over to see what the problem might be. The provider explained that the child had seen her pull up quite a while ago and was now questioning why she hadn't come in. She tried to explain the child's feelings and express to the mom just how much her child missed her all day, but the mom looked annoyed that she had ended an important conference call thinking something was actually wrong. Something was very wrong in deed, but the provider apologized and again tried to explain how this child was feeling. In the end, his mom abruptly responded by saying, "Don't worry about it. From now on, I will just honk and you can bring him out to me."

While this story is sad on many levels and there are a few lessons to be learned from it, the main point here is that daycares don't have drive-thrus for a reason, and honking will not get your child delivered to your car like a chocolate milkshake. You should be as excited to see your child as your child is to see you at the end of a long day. You should also look forward to spending a few minutes in his daycare checking out the latest art projects, chatting with your child's teacher and making your child feel like his home away from home is a place that is important to you too. As parents we tend to get so wrapped up in our own lives, jobs and everyday demands that we forget daycare is not a place of convenience where we can make deliveries and later order our kids to go. Kids will only be young once so enjoy these moments and make the extra time for them that they deserve. Go the extra mile, put forward a little more effort and every now and then, try to see life through their eyes. Convenience is a great thing we all love it but there's the right time and place for it, and pickup time at your child's daycare isn't one of them.

The Teeny Weeny Little Diapereeny

Every now and then, parents will donate diapers that have outgrown their children, and usually these diapers are either newborn or size 1. They will be placed into a bin labeled "extra" to be used as emergency backup when a child is completely out of diapers. These tiny diapers could be squeezed onto a baby of a bigger size, if needed, but trying to squeeze them onto a toddler is definitely pushing it!

The parent of a toddler had been reminded several times that her child had only enough diapers left for a week. Either the parent never picked up her child's reminder notes, or just kept forgetting to bring in more diapers, but by the end of the week, the child was out. After the teacher used the last diaper that morning, she called his mom and left a message but did not receive a call back. After a couple hours, this child's diaper needed changing again.

Now, not only was this child a toddler, but a larger and hefty one at that! When the teacher was preparing to change his diaper, she had no choice but to request a diaper from the Infant Room's "extra" stash. This meant the diaper would be many sizes too small and she would probably end up needing help to get it on him. As the teacher held the teeny diaper in place on the child, barely covering the necessities, the assistant used masking tape to try to bring the two sides of the diaper together. The diaper kept popping out on one side, then the other, until they finally got it under control and all taped up! The child ended up with what looked like a teeny bikini diaper, Brazilian style! As we watched the child standing their proudly looking like a tiny sumo wrestler, we realized the situation was funny and unfortunate all at the same time, but the child didn't seem to mind and at least the "situation" was covered.

One of the few requests providers continuously have is for parents to remember to bring in more diapers and wipes. You may be inconvenienced by a phone call at work but imagine how your child may feel in a diaper that is many sizes too small, or not to be changed at all. It always makes providers wonder what parent's think we will use if their child is out of diapers? We are daycares after all, not 24 hour convenience stores!

No, We Do Not Deliver!

A six-week-old baby had just started attending a home daycare which was conveniently located just across the street from his house. His parents had him at a later stage of their lives and had been feeling a bit overwhelmed by his arrival so they were very relieved to find a daycare close by and be able to return to work and the normalcy of everyday life shortly after. The daycare provider was happy to take the baby and was optimistic about the arrangement with her neighbors.

At first, the parents would dutifully come to pick the child up at 3:30 on their way home from work. The baby was doing great and seemed very happy with the provider and soon the parents began picking the child up later and later. As spring arrived and the weather became warmer, the daycare provider started noticing his parents sitting outside on their patio, sipping drinks, while she was still caring for their child. At first this was no big deal, but after several weeks of watching this child's parents sit outside for hours after work and relax while she was caring for their new born baby, she became very frustrated and felt they were taking advantage of the situation.

One afternoon, feeling like she'd had enough, she put the baby, who was the only child left, in his stroller and walked him by his house in hopes that his parents would get the hint and want to take their child. As she walked by their house, they casually waved at her, which she thought was odd, but they never got up or stopped their conversation to come see the baby at all.

At 5:30, which was closing time, his parents finally walked over to get the baby and casually explained to the provider that if she was going to walk the baby again near closing time, she could feel free to drop him off at their home if she wanted to. This was appalling and heartbreaking to the provider, mainly because she knew these parents were missing out on precious time with their sweet little boy, which we all know goes by way too quickly! Unfortunately, they were much too focused on the convenience factor instead.

Most children, within a reasonably short amount of time, will adjust to the routine of daycare and become comfortable in their daycare setting. Parents are usually very relieved to show up after work and find their children happily playing with friends or engaged in activities. As great as this is, some parents often mistake this to mean that their children don't miss them while they are gone. As daycare providers, we want to assure you that your kids do miss you very much while you are away from them. They know by the scheduled activity what time their parents typically arrive and they eagerly watch each parent as they walk through the door, hoping their own will show up next. We understand, at times, it's easier to get some errands done before coming to pick up your child, but this shouldn't become a regular occurrence and your child shouldn't always be the last one to be picked up.

The Haircut That Never Happened

The main reason I decided to own and operate a childcare center was that I hold children and their well-being very close to my heart. Having a soft spot for children, my staff and I have gone above and beyond the call of duty many times when we felt a family needed a helping hand. Unfortunately, sometimes that kindness gets taken for granted and, worse yet, gets abused.

A single mother of three had all three kids attending my daycare for several years. At times, throughout the years, the mother had car trouble or other things that prevented her from picking up her children. Since she lived very close to the center, one of the teachers or I would drop her children off each time one of these isolated incidents occurred.

At one point, one of her children required a surgical procedure, and I offered to bring her other two children to the hospital at the end of the day since I planned on visiting her child anyway. At the end of my visit, I offered to take her other children back home with me to sleep over so she could stay overnight with her child at the hospital. It's not unusual for providers to develop close bonds with the children and families they work with, and treat those children as if they were their own. The night went well and in the morning, I brought the children back to daycare. Later that afternoon, their mother came to pick them up, and all returned to normal.

Many months later, the mother called me one morning and asked me to please take her oldest child for a haircut because he had school pictures scheduled the next day. I couldn't really believe what I was hearing! I told her I didn't have the time to take my own child for a haircut, let alone someone else's! I was taken aback and felt truly disrespected by her request. To make matters worse, when I arrived at daycare later that morning, the office assistant handed me the cash the mother had dropped off earlier for me to pay for the haircut. How presumptuous of her!

Providers can and will make exceptions as needed for the children they care for and for the families that they serve. However, please remember that our jobs as providers are no less busy than other jobs; in fact, our jobs can be busier, and caring for children's lives can require a higher level of responsibility than other jobs. That a parent would assume we have time to run her or his personal errands would be comical if it weren't so insulting. Whether it's to drive a child to a regularly scheduled lesson or an occasional appointment, make sure you have an agreement with your provider about special requests above and beyond their standard services.

6.

At Last...

Or Is This Really Just the Beginning?

Now that we have opened your eyes and expanded your horizons to the daycare world, we hope you feel more confident that a successful outcome is indeed possible, but it will require time and effort to find it. You can now recognize the important things to consider versus areas where you can compromise. You are now empowered and encouraged to use your voice to speak up and make your opinions and concerns known; after all, if you don't, who will? But one of the more important lessons we've attempted to share, which we hope you truly understood, is that perfection doesn't exist – not in daycare nor in life.

Eventually finding the ideal daycare and getting off to a successful start can be a joyous experience, and certainly one to celebrate, but don't be fooled into thinking that your job is done. Stay diligent and be involved in your child's daycare to continue making it a positive and successful experience. Like many relationships, the one with your daycare

provider may hit some bumps along the way, and when it does, it's great to be prepared and know what steps to take. Being comfortable with your child's caregivers, and communicating openly and honestly with them, will leave you with much-needed peace of mind and make this transition easier. On the other hand, always keep a vigilant eye out for red flags, including changes in your child's behavior, which might be indicative of possible issues at daycare. And most importantly, you need to listen. Listen to what your child is saying about daycare and listen to your intuition. If something doesn't feel right, it probably means it isn't. If your child is too young to communicate, pay attention to body language when handing your child over to his caregiver and likewise, notice his demeanor when you pick him up.

With your eyes now wide open, and with a greater understanding and appreciation for the daycare world, we hope you are more prepared and able to trust in this journey and also to better handle any "bumps" in the road or challenges along the way.

Momma in Tears

 My favorite phone calls to receive at my daycare center are those from new mothers. I'm just so excited for them! I love congratulating them and asking them how parenthood feels, which often takes me back to the joyous moments when I had my first baby. The problem is, most of the new moms are usually in tears when they call.

I was at my center one afternoon when the phone started ringing, which the office assistant normally answers. By the fourth ring, it was clear the assistant was too busy to answer it and voice mail would kick in, so I shot out of my chair and rushed for the phone, practically tripping along the way! On the line was a new mom looking for daycare for her newborn, but the tone of her voice said it all – she was *not* happy about it. She explained that she had been calling daycares all morning, and to her dismay, she was not hearing or feeling what she had hoped for, and this was going to be her last daycare call.

She started off by asking the general questions most parents ask regarding hours of operation, tuition cost and available openings. I sensed that something was bothering her so I asked if she was okay, and that's when the floodgates burst open! Talking through tears, she stated she was losing hope because the centers she had called so far sounded very cold and unwelcoming. She didn't want to even tour them let alone consider leaving her infant there and she was becoming more uneasy about this situation each and every day.

I began to speak to her not as a director, but as one parent to another, and told her how I completely understood where she was coming from. I first assured her that every fear and doubt she was feeling was normal and to be expected. She *should* be nervous about leaving her child with a complete stranger! One of the main reasons I opened my own center was because I couldn't imagine leaving my own infant in someone else's care. Now here I was, telling parents why they should leave their children with *me*. I shared my beliefs on what a quality childcare program should offer, and how particular I was about the people I hired and the high standards and expectations I had set for myself and my center.

As I do with all parents, I asked her questions about her situation and her needs, her fears about daycare, and whether it was by choice or by necessity so she would be returning to work. These questions allow me to better understand each situation and be able to address each parent's specific needs and concerns. In this mom's case, she was devastated to have to go back to work and leave her baby, but because her household required a two-person income, it wasn't a realistic option for her to quit her job and stay home. As we conversed further and I answered more of her questions, I could hear the tone of her voice changing as she felt more at ease and began to trust me. At the end of our (30-minute) conversation, it seemed she had finally found someone she could talk to and, at last, she might actually trust her baby in a daycare center after all.

I don't think there's anything worse than having to leave your little one due to necessity instead of choice, but that's the reality for many. The best thing to do then is to find a place that feels most like a second home to you and your child. When you call daycares, you really should feel like the person you're initially speaking with cares about your situation and gives you the time you need. When you set up a tour, request more time if desired. During the tour, pay attention to the way the staff as well as the environment make you feel. Trust your instincts and listen to your intuition. The right place is out there, it just might take a little while longer to find it than you expected.

"Bumps" In the Road...

Have you ever received a frantic call from a close friend or family member and you immediately realize it is your job to just listen, whether you agree or disagree, and not say a word? I recently received such a call from one of my closest friends who lives in another state. We don't talk very often but when we do, the conversation usually leads to our children and this time was no different.

I received her call while I was in the middle of a hundred things but, when I heard her tone, I knew she needed my attention. She was clearly very upset and angry and, as I tried to figure out the problem, she blurted out, "I never should have taken him to that place! He is out of there! What are they doing all day while they are NOT watching my baby! I'm paying them a fortune and for what, a bruised child?!" I continued to listen to her steady stream of ranting and raving and the only thing I could clearly figure out was that something had obviously happened at her son's new daycare and someone was obviously going to hear about it!

After a few minutes, I finally got the chance to ask her what had happened. I knew her son had just started daycare a few weeks ago at a place she'd come to believe was "perfection". She had just recently spoken so highly of this new daycare that I couldn't believe she was now referring to the same place. She had been so impressed with the staff, the security, the lesson plans and the location. As soon as her son had started at his new daycare, she told me about the daily pictures and updates she had received from the director and how much they had reaffirmed her decision. What could possibly have gone so wrong?

She finally calmed down and stated that her son, who had just turned 2, had come home with a big bump on his forehead. I waited for the rest of the horrible story but that was it. When I asked her to tell me more, she said she had received a call from the child's teacher telling her he had bumped his head. The teacher said he was fine and they had applied ice but they wanted her to be aware of it. When she had gone to pick him up an hour later she was shocked to see such a large bump and bruise on her child and it made her feel like a bad mom for leaving him in a place that would allow this to happen.

I now felt it was a good time to speak up and I asked her if she felt like someone had hurt her child, to which she replied, "Well, no." I then informed her that the daycare had done everything right. They had called her to let her know what had happened, and had treated the injury. I also reminded her that she had been consistently happy with the care that her son had been receiving and that kids were going to get occasional bumps and bruises no matter where they were or who they were with. I then asked her if her child had ever bumped his head at home. She quickly answered, "Of course, but I never expected him to get hurt at daycare, those people get paid just to watch kids."

My friend ended up taking her son back to that daycare the next day, but I think a good lesson was learned. Perfection doesn't exist anywhere...so don't kid yourself into thinking it can exist in daycare. You may find an excellent center or a quality home daycare but believe it or not, issues and incidents may still pop up. The challenge is, once they do, can you still see the big picture and realize how the event might have taken place, or will you run at the first sign of difficulty or danger without even considering the facts? If you choose the later, I suggest you invest in a good pair of running shoes...you will need them.

The Last Minute Phone Call

Just after dinner, a parent received a phone call from her child's daycare. She had her three-year-old twin boys at a center, and the director had spoken to her several times about their behavioral issues. Each time, she would listen and address the issues, hoping that things would get better. That night, when she answered the phone and heard the voice of the daycare center's owner, she guessed it wasn't going to be good. Well, it was even worse than she thought!

The director started the conversation by informing her it had been determined, by herself and her staff, the boys were a safety threat not only to the other children, but also to the staff. (We are talking about three-year-old boys here, mind you!) The mother was horrified, and confused as to why they considered the situation to be that extreme. When she had initially enrolled them at the center, the staff was very supportive and she felt good about her choice and hopeful that things would work out. Clearly, things were not working out as she had hoped. The owner went on to say that her children were not allowed to return the next morning and were being dismissed immediately. (Whereas *she* would have been required to give a two-week notice before withdrawing her children from the center, apparently it was within the center's policy to kick them out without any notice at all!) She stood there holding the phone in disbelief, feeling hurt and confused. She knew she would have to take the next day off of work to go gather her children's belongings from their old daycare and figure things out.

The next day she began asking friends and family for referrals to another daycare, and that's how I ended up on the phone with this mom later that afternoon. When I received her call, she was extremely shaken up and couldn't get through the conversation without crying. During our conversation, she agreed that her boys would fight sometimes, mainly with each other, but they were not the little monsters that the director of the previous center had described them to be. Her biggest worry was whether another center would even consider taking them after this incident. After getting to know her better and learning more about her sons and their situation, it was evident what an involved and concerned parent she was and I was hopeful that we could help her achieve better results than what she had just experienced.

The next morning she arrived with her sons and we were all expecting something completely different! We were prepared for the worst and even had a plan in place to protect the other children if her sons got out of control. What we didn't expect to see were these two tiny little boys who immediately won our hearts with their big eyes and exuberant personalities. They quickly had us hooked on every word they spoke, and boy did they speak a lot!

Over the course of the next few days, weeks and months, these children transformed their behavior from one extreme to the other and eventually became completely manageable. As their mom had originally warned, they did fight, but it was almost always with each other. Initially, it took a little extra time and effort to get them accustomed to our rules and expectations but soon enough, they were considered to be "favorites" by many of the teachers. Their mother was in tears again, but this time it was tears of joy. She finally felt she had found the right place for them and was so thankful and overjoyed. We now have had them for over 2 years, and we continue to work with them when they have their "moments", but then again, we *all* have our "moments" too.

Sometimes it's not the children that need changing, but the environment. When children are directed in positive ways and trust their providers, they will be encouraged to change accordingly. If they feel they are being pushed against, they will push back. We have had many kids throughout the years that came to us with issues requiring extra patience and loving attention; fortunately, we had sufficient and competent staff to make this happen. Amazingly, it never takes long to see the positive changes in these children once they have created trusting bonds with their caregivers. No parent should ever feel like his or her child isn't as great or worthy as another's. The most important quality to look for in any good daycare is a commitment to helping parents find and bring out the best in each individual child, and to succeed in doing so no matter how challenging that task may turn out to be.

● ● ● ● ●

My center has gained a reputation over the years of being the center that takes all the "unwanted" children. I actually take that as a compliment, because once we take them under our wings and believe they can change, we see magic happen! One should never give up on children. A caregiver's role is so powerful, and when you find the right players for your child's team, you can look forward to his success.

● ● ● ● ●

Monkeying Around

You don't always really know how or when you may stumble upon something that you've been looking for, but when you do, it's pretty exciting. In some cases, you may not even know you were looking for something until it's right there in front of you and it has actually found *you*.

During long summer days, I would often take my small group of daycare kids to a really fun park near my home. This park was a favorite of the kids. We usually enjoyed a picnic under the large trees, then spent hours having races, swinging, and playing on the large climbers built in the shape of a police car and a fire engine. The monkey bars were also popular, so I would spend a lot of time either holding kids up to help them across or showing them tricks like hanging upside down, which the kids loved. A great thing about playing at the park was that the kids would try new things as they played together. Many times, other kids joined us as their moms or daycare providers sat and watched from benches, looking bored or talking on their phones.

One day as we were playing, I noticed a group of office workers eating lunch outside, enjoying the warm day. After a while, they all went back to their air-conditioned offices, but one stayed outside and continued to watch us. I was busy showing kids how to hang upside down on the monkey bars and hold hands when I heard someone nearby say, "Excuse me…" I looked around and noticed the woman from the office building standing close by looking up at me with wonder and amusement, as I'm sure it's not often one sees a 40-year-old hanging upside down. I jumped down and turned to her and she started to laugh and asked me if all of the kids were mine or if I ran a daycare. I assured her that while I may have appeared to be crazy, the kids were not all mine and yes, I ran a daycare. She then told me that she had been watching us play all summer long from her office window and she wished her kids were having this much fun at their daycare also. She ended up asking for my number and inquired if I would consider enrolling her three-year-old daughter.

The funny part of this story is that this mom was not looking for a daycare, since she was content with what she had…until she happened to find something different and realized it's what she'd rather have. This happens quite often in life, as well as in daycare, and it really makes you aware of the importance of exploring your options before making a choice. Keep your priority list in mind while searching, and don't settle until you find exactly what you're looking for, because it does exist. Often times, the hardest part of the journey is finding that ideal place for your child, but when your search is over and that "perfect" place is found, you'll realize that it was all worth it. Keep your eyes as well as your mind wide open, because you never know when that ideal place might just be right in front of you!

Section II:

The Childcare Providers

Childcare is a highly misunderstood, overlooked and greatly underappreciated occupation. It is not a coveted occupation that comes with a lot of acknowledgment or respect. In fact, providers are often referred to as "babysitters". Many think childcare is an easy job that just about anyone can do, but in reality, that is far from the truth. Just as we are all not cut out to be astronauts, pilots, doctors or lawyers, the same is true for childcare providers. This is a profession that requires a special knack for working with children all day, having extraordinary patience, the ability to multi-task, and a deep passion, love and understanding for children and their development.

From the outside, it may look quite simple: you drop your child off with their provider, they wave goodbye to you, and off to work you go. Then at pickup time, you greet your child, you are told they had a fun day, you say thank you, and off you go again to begin your busy nightly routine of being a parent. Do you ever stop to think about all of the things that are happening at daycare during that time? Do you appreciate all the work your provider is doing which allows you to work and earn a living in the first place?

A typical day for a childcare provider consists of many things, and for the most part, no two days are ever alike. One thing that does remain consistent is the magnitude of responsibility they are given in caring for children's lives. Despite all the demands that come with this responsibility, childcare providers are the last to be thanked for their services but the first to be blamed when an issue arises with a child. We want to offer due recognition to the childcare providers that show up, day after day, and perform a job that can be very mentally, emotionally and physically exhausting. They perform this job, sometimes with long hours and low pay, because they are passionate about working with children and they love what they do! Their real payback is the smiles they see on the children's faces they work with, and the positive impact they know they've helped make in their lives.

Each new day will bring a new set of challenges but great providers will greet you with a fresh smile, renewed energy and positive attitude, ready to inspire, educate and entertain your child all over again. Providers who do this from the heart and with the right intentions are absolutely priceless.

The following true stories will give an accurate portrayal of this profession from the daycare provider's perspective. These stories will take you "behind the scenes" and into the minds of providers to uncover valuable, eye-opening information parents can learn from. These stories will not only reveal the positive impact the right daycare provider can have on a child, but they will also highlight the negative impact a poor daycare provider can have on a child as well.

7.

All That Glitters Is Not Gold…

Are you choosing your daycare for all the right reasons?

W e've all been there…You're walking through the mall on a Sunday afternoon and you spot them – the perfect pair of shoes. You must have them! You don't consider how much they cost or if they will be comfortable or even if you have anything in your closet to match them. You just need them based on their appearance so you quickly rush into the store where you blurt out your size to the first store clerk that grabs your attention. The next thing you know, you are on your way home with the perfect pair of shoes and the thought suddenly enters your mind: *Did I make a good choice?*

Oddly enough, the same principles apply to just about anything, including daycare. Many parents can be impressed by expensive play structures, fancy buildings or (for home daycares) the nicest homes on the block. First impressions could fool us by making us believe if something looks a certain way, then it must *be* a certain way. We believe we'll get what we pay for in terms of quality, but the reality is: *all that glitters is not gold.* Choosing a daycare should never be a spur-of-the-moment decision or a decision based on appearance or convenience. The outside appearance may be very different from what's actually happening on the inside, and your child may not actually be receiving the level of care you were promised upon enrollment.

The question then is, how can you determine the level of quality care being provided after just a brief visit of a provider's home or daycare center? The answer can only come by thoroughly checking out the facility or home, asking the right questions, following up with surprise visits, and really trusting your instincts. You must learn to be the ultimate appraiser of your child's daycare and choose someone you feel you can trust your child's life with.

Culture Shock

A mom with two young boys had just moved to a quiet suburb in California from Spain. She had never needed to look for daycare before, but soon found herself with a new job and the need to find someone to care for her children, FAST! She asked some of the neighbors for good recommendations and was given one for a small daycare center that was close by. After driving by that center and noticing it looked quite run down, she dismissed that option. She soon noticed a home daycare that was on her way to work that looked beautiful, with a backyard full of playground equipment and toys, surrounded by a new chain-link fence. She called the daycare and was told they had openings and the boys could start the following week. The next day, after a brief interview, the mom was so impressed with the house, the yard and the activities that she enrolled her boys and felt good about her decision.

The following week, the boys started at the daycare and everything seemed to be going fine at first. The boys talked about the activities they did but they also complained about "Ken". They explained that he was mean and he sometimes pulled their hair. The mom was not very concerned, knowing that boys were often rough with each other, so she didn't give their story much thought, but they continued to complain about "Ken".

One Friday afternoon, the mom had a cancellation in her schedule and decided to pick the boys up early as a surprise. When she got to the daycare, the kids were playing outside. Walking around to the back of the house, she couldn't find her daycare provider anywhere but noticed a large man sitting under a tree smoking a cigarette! She walked over to him and asked who he was and why Judy, the provider, wasn't watching the kids. He grumbled to her that he was Ken, Judy's husband, and that Judy had gone to run errands while he was watching the kids.

Needless to say, the mom was completely shocked and horrified that something like this could ever happen. The daycare provider had never told her that someone else would ever be watching her kids, nor had she ever been introduced to the provider's husband. She reported the incident to licensing and pulled the boys out immediately and placed them in a daycare center where they have all been very happy. The mom felt so much guilt and shame after this incident but admitted that she never even thought to ask these important questions.

Incidents like this probably happen a lot more than you'd think. Knowing what to look for and asking the right questions can keep them from happening to your child. When choosing a childcare center or home daycare for your child, the things you can see during your visit are important, but they don't tell the whole story. When looking for childcare, ask your provider if anyone else will ever be interacting with your child and, if the answer is yes, insist on meeting them and on knowing when they will be watching your child. While a good referral from someone using the same daycare may set your mind at ease, make sure you stay involved and continue to form your own conclusion.

Tell-Tale Signs...

It makes sense to assume that a clean, well-kept daycare facility with smiling and attentive staff would be a safe place for a child. Parents tend to make choices based on what looks and feels right to them, but what happens when red flags appear that indicate otherwise? When unsettling events occur and things just don't seem to add up, parents must begin asking questions... which is how the truth in this next story was revealed.

A couple had enrolled their toddler at a highly recommended daycare center that looked clean and safe, and had a history of operating chains across the country for over 40 years. They liked the director and also felt a connection with the staff, all of whom seemed kind and trustworthy, including their child's teacher. Everything seemed to be going fine for the first few weeks until one evening, while bathing their little boy, his parents noticed strange-looking tiny bumps on his back. When they asked their child about them, he said it was from his teacher. His parents became concerned and the next day, while dropping their child off in his classroom, they again asked him about the bumps and he quickly pointed to a container of thumb tacks sitting on a counter. Becoming increasingly alarmed, rather than drop their child off, they immediately went over to the director's office. After hearing the parent's concerns, the director seemed shocked but defended the teacher, claiming the teacher would never do such a thing. She concluded that the teacher was probably using the thumb tacks to do an art project and the young child was probably confused. This explanation did not satisfy the confused parents, who suspected the bumps were from daycare, so they decided to also question the teacher. Not surprisingly, the teacher denied having any knowledge of this situation and seemed insulted to have even been questioned. At this point, the parents no longer trusted the teacher and were convinced she was harming their child, so they immediately removed him from the center and contacted a lawyer, as well as licensing.

During the investigation, a former employee came forward and testified that the teacher had used corporal punishment to discipline some of the toddlers on several occasions. She also stated that the teacher would take some children into the closet, and spank their bottoms and pinch their cheeks. This former employee claimed to have brought these accusations to the director's attention on more than one occasion but nothing was ever done about it, so she had quit her job shortly thereafter. These parents, along with several other families who had their children in that center, were saddened and in disbelief that this kind of thing could happen. Such incidents can leave parents questioning their judgment and wondering how they can trust again, especially when the reality of what they received was so different than their initial impression.

Unfortunately, this is not an isolated case of abuse or mistreatment of a child by someone who is later clearly shown to be unfit to serve as a childcare provider. When you turn your child over to another's care, there is never a guarantee they will be loved and nurtured in the way that you would hope. The good news is, there are many things you can do to know more about what's really going on in your child's daycare. First, before enrolling your child at your chosen center or home, ask if you can come back to spend a few hours there with your child. We highly recommend staying away from anywhere that doesn't allow you to do this. Second, once your child is enrolled, you should plan on popping in on your child unannounced at random times on different days, especially within the first few weeks of enrollment.

If you can, spend some extra time during drop-off and pick-up watching how the classroom operates, and what the other children's demeanors are like—especially around the teachers. If you don't see happy children, busy with activities, something is wrong. Most importantly, follow your intuition! If you feel like something is "off" in your child's daycare environment, then it probably is. Don't be afraid to ask questions and check things out. It's your job as a parent to know what is happening to your child as much as possible. These tools may never give you 100% peace of mind about your child's care and safety, but they will certainly give you a better idea of what is really going on at their daycare.

Not the Place for My Child!

Childcare providers typically have the unique advantage of either bringing their children to work with them if they work in a daycare center, or being at home with their children if they run a home daycare. As providers, with the inside knowledge that we have, we can be apprehensive about placing them in someone else's daycare. The following illustrates a case of a seemingly great home daycare that I would have actually considered.

Several years ago, my children and I had been invited to the home of a friend who ran a home daycare, and had been doing so for 20 years. She had a big, beautiful house with an impressive playground and outside area, and she often did fun and creative activities with her daycare kids. That day, she had set up a gigantic water slide and sprinkler which the kids loved, and everyone was having a great time. We spent several hours watching the kids play, run, swing and slide. After a while, the kids all enjoyed a snack of fruit and popsicles together. I remember thinking to myself that if I had to put my kids in daycare, this would be a good one because it seemed that my friend truly loved and cared about the children in her care.

After we had been there for about 3 hours, a van pulled up her long driveway and she asked me to keep an eye on the kids as she quickly ran inside. I really didn't think a thing about it until she returned a few minutes later holding a very young baby. With a big smile, she walked over to the mom who had just pulled in and started to talk about what a great day her baby had been having. The mom seemed pleased and was happy to see her baby. I suddenly thought to myself, *Where has this baby been all this time?!*

After the mom drove away, I questioned my friend about who had been watching the baby. She very casually responded that the baby had been napping, yet she hadn't gone into the house the entire time I was there. Since she didn't have a baby monitor outside with us, I was rather confused… how did she know that this baby was OK when no one seemed to be watching him for several hours? I continued to ask her if anyone else was in the house with the baby and, becoming annoyed, she mentioned that her teen age son was at home playing video games. At this point I dropped the subject and we left shortly thereafter.

This experience left me thinking that if I, as a provider, was thinking this was a great daycare, surely many parents would think that as well. The truth was that even though she was kind and loving around the kids, did a wonderful job of entertaining them, and seemed to have all the right equipment, a great act of negligence was committed here: a very young baby was left alone for several hours in a crib with little to no supervision. His mom picked him up and never even thought to ask the provider about her child's day.

As the old saying goes, if something seems too good to be true, it often is. We really want parents to think outside the box when analyzing their own daycare situations and to ask questions when things are not making sense. Have you ever asked your home daycare provider how the older kids can go outside if the younger ones are sleeping? Does she use baby monitors when kids are asleep? Does she ever send the older kids outside to play unattended? These are important questions to ask because events such as this happen all too often. When it comes to your childcare services, you are paying for a certain level of care and should demand it; if you're not receiving it, it's time to start looking elsewhere because it does exist.

While Cameras Roll...

Some daycare centers look very top-notch and elite with fancy camera equipment and high-tech security cards required to enter the building. These centers generally come with a huge price tag for tuition as well. In some cases, you are certainly getting what you pay for, but at times is high quality care simply assumed based  on expensive objects and elaborate surroundings? When it comes down to it, what really matters above and beyond anything else is the care and the love your child receives. Don't be fooled into thinking staff can always be trusted just because cameras exist in a classroom. I personally know this isn't true since I used cameras when I first opened my daycare center and definitely didn't get the results I expected. I not only thought the cameras would be a great selling point to families that toured, but they would also be an easy way to keep teachers focused on their jobs. Although the cameras did impress the parents that toured, they simply did not impress me...

I had a teacher in the Infant room that had her own baby in the class with her. (I try to avoid hiring teachers to work in the same classrooms as their children, but it can't always be avoided.) During orientation, she was specifically informed about our policy regarding staff children which states that when a teacher is working in the same classroom as her child, the other staff members are required to care for that child as much as possible. I began noticing whenever I passed through her room that she would be caring for her own child more often than not, and ignoring the others. Whenever I questioned her, she would either say she had just picked up her own baby a minute ago, or that the other teachers were busy so she had no choice but to tend to her own baby's needs. I didn't believe this could be a coincidence each time it happened, but I respected this teacher and wanted to believe her, so I gave her the benefit of the doubt.

A few weeks later, my suspicions were confirmed when other teachers, as well as two parents that had babies in the infant room, came to me with more complaints. At this point, I decided I would watch the camera in the infant room more diligently to see what was actually happening. I had assumed that since the staff knew there were cameras in the classrooms, they would naturally behave more conscientiously and follow policies at all times. I was wrong. The more time I spent watching that specific camera, the more I saw this teacher carrying, feeding and mainly playing with just her baby. I was truly surprised and realized that the presence of a camera didn't matter to her one bit. When confronted again, she tried to deny it and make more excuses despite my telling her what the cameras revealed. She was let go immediately and I eventually got rid of the cameras. Instead, I preferred to monitor classrooms by walking through them more frequently throughout the day, instead of sitting in my office watching monitors. This also gave me the chance to experience more special little moments with all the children in the center. Between myself, the assistant director and the office assistant, we walk through the various classrooms a lot, and I feel in this way we truly get to see an accurate picture!

There are many shocking cases of nannies and childcare providers performing abusive or neglectful acts, right in front of cameras knowing they were being videotaped! This leads me to believe that a provider, or anyone for that matter, will show their true colors eventually, whether cameras are present or not. If a childcare provider is not cut out for the demands of the job, a camera isn't going to change that. Ultimately, we, as parents, are the best eyes, ears and advocates for our children, so rely on your intuition more than the false comfort you think a security camera will provide.

● ● ● ● ●

Once while watching the cameras, I noticed a staff member not moving for a while, so I got up to go check on her in the classroom... She was asleep!

● ● ● ● ●

8.

The Job of a Superhero...

Can your provider be the superhero you've been looking for?

Who doesn't love a superhero? They swoop in at the very last second and save the world from imminent disaster using their extraordinary powers and skill. They can leap tall buildings with a single bound, fly faster than the speed of light and rescue people from dangerous situations all in the blink of an eye! Each superhero has his or her own unique abilities but what makes them all super is that they sacrifice their own needs, while placing the needs of others first.

Many professions have what can be considered superheroes working amongst them. Many people consider police and firemen to be superheroes as they risk their lives each day to help others. Doctors and nurses can also be considered superheroes as they use their training and practiced skill to save the lives of the people we love.

Daycare providers, like superheroes, do a job each day that requires superhuman skills to perform, and they are rarely acknowledged for their ability to handle tough situations under pressure. A daycare provider must possess extraordinary powers of patience, persistence, resistance, the ability to read minds and be able to super multi-task constantly. Like Superman, they are responsible for the welfare and safety of those in their care… but wait, Superman never had to deal with biting toddlers, diaper blow-outs, and projectile vomiting of breast milk in his face while trying to save the world! That makes the villains he had to fight seem like nothing in comparison!

Daycare providers can calm several crying babies at once, get a toddler room full of 14 two-year-olds to sleep, get 20 preschoolers to follow directions, and they can cook lunch, sing songs and play games all at the same time. Daycare providers work tirelessly each day, using their unique skills and talents to teach and care for children while also keeping them safe and entertained. They may not be able to fly but watch them reach a falling child with the speed of light. They may not have super-sonic hearing, but they can hear a baby cry and know exactly from the sound of it what that baby needs. Finally, they may not have ESP, but their intuition will tell them very quickly when something is not right and needs attention. Most daycare providers have extraordinary gifts when it comes to working with children and these gifts qualify them as superheroes. It's time they were recognized for their talents and skills, and given the credit they deserve!

Daycare Diva Saves the Day

Through the years, at my center, we have worked with a lot of children that required some extra attention. Contrary to what one might think, most times these are the children we tend to bond closer with, and really see the fruits of our labor as we see their behavior improve over time. One boy in particular, who had started at the age of two, had a very hard time controlling his anger. As a toddler, he would throw screaming fits and knock toys off shelves, but as he grew older, his rages became much more serious and violent, sometimes requiring us to hold him down in a bear hug to prevent him from hurting himself or others. With extreme behavioral issues, we make an effort to help the child improve only if the family is also willing to work with us as a team in achieving our desired goal. Part of this agreement involves the parent being available to pick up their child when called at a moment's notice whenever we feel the child's behavior is beyond what we can handle. We continued to work with him and his family in trying different methods to improve his behavior. He had some great days along the way, and some not-so-great days…

Three years later, about 6 months before starting Kindergarten, he began doing consistently well at the center and his behavior had drastically improved. He had adapted to a routine we laid out for him that was working really well, so when Kindergarten was just around the corner, we were all very nervous about how he would do, knowing change was hard for him to handle.

We informed his Kindergarten teacher about the methods we used to help him control his outbursts, and he did okay during his first few weeks, then later started having some rough days here and there. One day I was scheduled to do a van run, which involved picking him up with several other children that attended the same school. When I arrived at his school, I became concerned when this child didn't come out to the van right away with the rest of the group. We waited and soon the Principal came over to tell me they were having trouble getting this child to come out, and he was in the office. They had tried contacting his mother but couldn't get a hold of her. I asked the Principal if he would like me to go in and try to get him out. He looked at me reluctantly and said, "Sure, you can try if you think it might help." He stayed and monitored the other children in the van while I went inside to assess the situation, thinking to myself, *I hope I can get him to come out.*

I found him in the main office with his shoes off, which he had thrown at the office staff, and he was full of rage and he just kept yelling "NO, NO, NO, NO!" He and I had had many moments together in the past which most times ended successfully with him giving me a hug, then returning to his preschool class, so I was hoping this would be one of those times. I decided that given the situation, I must act with confidence and swiftness. I walked over to him, quickly scooped him up in my arms, and with a big smile, said "Let's go, the other kids are looking for you", acting as if nothing was wrong. Even though he continued saying, "NO", he didn't fight me while he was in my arms so I was hopeful (but not positive yet) that this would turn out fine. Then I set him back down, helped him gather his shoes and put them on, and then grabbed his backpack. I took his hand, and as we headed toward the door, I apologized to the office ladies, who were watching in amazement. (I did ask if he would apologize to them also, but when he shook his head and began yelling, "NO" again, I decided not to push it. It's good to know which battles to fight, and which to surrender.) When the Principle saw us coming out, his jaw dropped! He looked at me and said, "what do you have, super powers?" I must admit, I felt pretty great at that moment. I looked at him and casually replied with a smile, "Maybe, or maybe I just got lucky."

Childcare providers do more than just "watch" children. They form bonds with them and act as a secondary family to the children and families they serve. It gives us great joy when we see the progress the children we care for make through the years. With all that we are challenged with and still strive to accomplish each day, we consider it, 'All in A Day's Work' in the life of a Daycare Superhero!

Field Trip to the Emergency Room

One super power that many daycare providers wish for is the ability to foresee future events. If we could only anticipate when a normal, sunny, summer day would suddenly take a tragic turn, we might be better prepared for it, or better yet, avoid it in the first place.

On a sunny, warm day, a home daycare provider was watching a group of mainly older pre-school children happily riding bikes in her driveway and drawing pictures on her sidewalk with chalk. Her six-year-old son was among them and he happened to be sitting on his older brother's bike teetering back and forth trying to ride it. She was not very concerned as her son was an adventurous boy who often climbed, jumped, and rode things that were too big for his small size. Suddenly she heard him cry out in pain! As she quickly ran to him, she noticed a large amount of blood soaking through the back of his shorts. Analyzing the situation, she discovered that when the bike tipped sideways, the kickstand had punctured the back of his leg, causing a large cut, from which blood was rapidly seeping!

At this point, the daycare provider flew into panic mode and without thinking she grabbed her son, took off his shirt and tightly tied it around his leg. She then put him into a car seat and tightly buckled him in. Next she grabbed the other children, who were standing in the driveway covered in chalk, and one by one buckled them in the van as well. Once everyone was in, she then ran into the house, grabbed her keys and took off for the emergency room.

A few minutes later they arrived at the emergency room and the daycare provider pulled up to the front door and loudly beeped the horn. Within a minute, a nurse appeared and offered her assistance. The provider explained the situation and told the nurse to get a wheel chair. The nurse quickly obliged and the provider lifted her son into the chair and noticed the alarming amount of blood that now covered the shirt as well as the car seat. She was terrified, but remained in control, as the nurse quickly wheeled her son through the doors of the hospital.

The provider then parked the car and walked all the kids into the hospital waiting room. Once they were all seated, she realized she had forgotten her cell phone and could not contact parents to inform them of the situation. She knew she needed to be with her son, who was probably even more terrified without her, so she asked the receptionist to call her mom and ask her to come to the hospital to stay with the kids.

The provider's mom soon arrived at the hospital with some crackers, juice boxes, and coloring books. The provider ran off to check on her son who she found screaming, yelling and fighting with the doctors as they tried to mend his leg. A lot of struggling and 26 stitches later, they were finally ready to leave the hospital and go back home.

That evening, as parents came to pick up their kids, the provider filled them in on the events of the day and they were all so very shocked! They couldn't believe what she had been through and how well she had handled it all with so many children to care for. They all agreed that they probably would not have known what to do if they had been in the same situation and they commended her for keeping calm and thinking straight in such a stressful situation.

Being a daycare provider or a superhero means never knowing when tragedy is going to strike. It requires the special ability to drop everything at a moment's notice and react to an emergency while still putting the safety and well-being of others first. You must think on the run and make tough choices and split-second decisions that could affect lives. It's not a job for the weak at heart and as any good superhero knows, we do it all for the sake of others. It's what being a good superhero or daycare provider is all about.

All Aboard the Vomit Express!

Everyone occasionally has what they consider to be a "bad" day at the office. If your office happens to be a home daycare, then a "bad" day can mean a variety of things. When the illness commonly known as rotavirus enters a home daycare, a bad day suddenly takes on a whole new meaning and a provider must channel his or her inner "superhero" FAST!

Rotavirus is a common and highly contagious form of stomach flu that spreads very quickly and causes young children to experience severe vomiting and very bad diarrhea. If it hits one child, be prepared for it to quickly hit the rest, as I found out the hard way in my own home daycare…

What started as a baby not wanting his breakfast and running a low-grade temperature, quickly turned into that same baby vomiting on the carpet and filling diaper after diaper with the worst diarrhea I had ever seen or smelled. I quickly called his mom then tried to keep up on his changings until she arrived, when the next child started to vomit and soon was also having severe stomach pains and diarrhea.

Before noon that day, several more children were throwing up in bowls and buckets and I was bathing and changing kids almost constantly! I didn't stop running that day between washing, changing and scrubbing, while at the same time, trying to comfort and care for several sick children. Parents couldn't have arrived soon enough! One mom still recalled many years later how she walked in that day and saw me holding a baby in each arm, both vomiting on my floor.

That day was an absolute nightmare but daycare providers must be prepared for anything. They must do whatever it takes to care for the children whose parents have chosen them for the job. They ARE superheroes and when the time comes, they must put on their capes and rise to the challenge. The children in their care are counting on them!

● ● ● ● ●

I once decided to change my 16 month old baby's diaper in the front seat of the car, on my lap, while seven months pregnant. My husband wanted to go back into the restaurant to change her but I assured him that any supermom could quickly and efficiently change a diaper in a snap! Once done, I proudly placed her back in her car seat and we were set to go, or so I overconfidently thought. When we walked into Target ten minutes later, I felt wetness on the back of my pants leg, and reached for it only to end up with a piece of poo in my hands. Startled, I flung it in the air without thinking, and it landed on the floor with a splat! After returning from my mad dash to the bathroom to wash up, I was humiliated as workers had to quarantine a huge section at the front of the store to disinfect it, and I quietly made my exit back out of the store as inconspicuously as possible. Sometimes, even super heroes miss their mark!

• • • • •

Just In Time!

All childcare providers, both home and center, are required to be certified in First Aid and CPR. Now, it's one thing to go through the training, where you learn and practice on resuscitation dummies, and a whole other thing to actually put these skills into practice in real life. I can probably speak for many trained professionals when I say that we dread the day we may actually have to put what we've learned to use in real life. It can be both a paralyzing and a powerful feeling, as an assistant director of a center discovered...

It was a late summer afternoon and the day was coming to an end with an hour left before closing time. The assistant director was making her rounds through the classrooms when she arrived at the Toddler room. She noticed one of the little girls just didn't look right. Her complexion looked a little gray, then suddenly, right before her eyes she began turning blue! As she swiftly ran to her side, the little girl suddenly collapsed in her arms. She laid her down on the floor and tapped her to see if she was responsive; the child was completely unresponsive. The teacher thought to herself, *This can't be happening!* She leaned down to see if her chest was rising, and determined the child was not breathing. She yelled to the other teachers in the room, "She's unresponsive! Call 911!" The assistant director's heart was beating out of her chest as she prepared to begin CPR on this little girl, thinking, *I can do this.*

By this time the other teacher was on the phone with 911, and when they asked her for the center's address, she was so panicked that she couldn't remember it even though she had been working there for two years! Another parent had entered the room by then, and she also couldn't remember the address, but she pulled out the center's business card and blurted it out to the teacher on the phone. The emergency team was on its way!

Meanwhile, the assistant director had blown her first breath into the little girl, with no success. She repositioned the little girl's head and blew in another breath, this time, successfully. As anyone who's been CPR-trained knows, one good breath deserves another! After the second breath went in, before even having to begin compressions, the little girl suddenly came to. Oh heavens, what a relief! Within the next two minutes, the emergency team arrived, followed by the child's mother. The mother was grateful beyond words for the assistant director having saved her daughter's life. This was truly a superhero moment!

Later, the child's mom informed the staff involved that she had forgotten to tell them her child had a condition where her brain sometimes forgets to tell her to breathe, so she had experienced many fainting spells in the past. Wow, just a little (but significant) detail she forgot to mention!

Ultimately, the person you choose to care for your child is the person to whom you are entrusting your child's life. Make sure they are prepared and fully aware of how to handle emergency situations that may arise. Your child's provider will have to be their substitute superhero, while you, their main superhero, is away. Make sure they are certified and have the skills and training required for the job!

• • • • •

You may ask a provider to show you their First Aid and CPR cards, so you can ensure they are current. Most states require they be renewed every 2 to 3 years.

• • • • •

9.

It Drives Us Nuts…

How well can you do your job while being driven nuts?!

E very profession undoubtedly comes with a list of things that drives the members of that profession nuts! For instance, a dental hygienist must hate it when patients come in without brushing their teeth. Lawyers must go nuts when they discover at some point that their clients had lied or withheld important information or evidence. And it probably drives a shoe salesman nuts when women insist on trying size 7 shoes on their size 8 feet! Well, the same is true for daycare providers.

If parents were aware of our most common frustrations, and the sort of things that bother or offend us, they may make a more conscious effort to not have these issues occur as often. Ongoing efforts toward mutual respect and understanding between parent and provider is critical for creating the best daycare experience possible. Many of the following concerns and complaints can affect a provider's job performance, ultimately affecting the quality of the children's daycare experience. As parents, we are very busy trying to meet all our daily obligations. Just as you take the time to care for your work and home responsibilities, make sure you take the time to care for all your daycare responsibilities as well, and show the respect to your provider that they deserve.

• • • • •

As parents, remember the choice in becoming a parent means your life and schedule really does need to revolve around your child's needs. There's nothing more annoying than a parent who gets annoyed because their child's needs disrupted their day.

• • • • •

Can I Have Your Number?

A common frustration for daycare providers is when parents don't update their emergency information after they change jobs or phone numbers. It's especially crucial when we have a sick or injured child in our care with no way to reach the parent. In the event we do have the correct number and end up leaving a message, oftentimes, a call back may not be received in a timely manner.

One morning, a few hours after being dropped off, a preschool child was beginning to look uneasy and had shown disinterest in participating in any activities. When her teacher checked her temperature under her arm, it had already reached 102 degrees. She was laid down on a cot to rest with a cool rag on her forehead, while the staff tried to contact her mother. Calling her mother's cell phone resulted in a recorded message that said the number was no longer in service. Her work number was called next but no one answered, so the teacher left a message. Next, the emergency contacts were tried and finally, the second contact listed had an updated cellular number for the child's mother.

Meanwhile, the child's fever had spiked to 106 degrees, and she had started to quiver! The little girl was scared, and repeatedly kept asking for her mom. At this point the director decided to call 911, and the ambulance showed up within 5 minutes. Just as the emergency team entered, the child's mother was finally reached. She was informed about the situation and told to go to the hospital where the ambulance would take her child. She felt horrible when she realized she had changed her number a few weeks ago, and forgotten to update her child's information.

This type of situation unfortunately occurs quite frequently. As daycare providers, we cannot stress enough the importance of updating your phone numbers, job changes and emergency contacts as soon as they change. When the parent's information is not current, it will always be the child that suffers in the event that an accident, injury, or sickness occurs. If you can't receive direct phone calls at work, make sure you leave a number at work where a live person can be reached. If daycare is calling, it's usually serious, so make sure you can always be reached!

Panic on Payday!

Many years ago while working as the director at a busy daycare center, it was my responsibility to keep track of weekly tuition payments and to make daily deposits. Believe it or not, this was one of the most stressful parts of the job due to the fact that many parents did not make their weekly daycare payments a priority. One family in particular was always late with their weekly payment and would never say a word about it, which made the situation even more awkward. They drove a very expensive car, their kids always had the nicest clothes and shoes, but somehow paying for childcare was always on the bottom of their priority list.

After several written reminders, I finally had to confront the parents about their bill and I was rudely dismissed with a casual, "Oh, I forgot." "I will drop it off tomorrow." As a daycare provider and the director of the center, I felt like this parent was telling us how completely unimportant we were to her even though she showed up bright and early every morning with her two children. What else should we assume when a parent says they have forgotten to pay us? It's one thing when parents are struggling to pay due to their tight finances, but those parents usually tell us right away and we are happy to work with them. It's another situation when we are forgotten about and ignored over and over again, yet the children continue to show up. That is when we realize how little we our valued. We often want to ask in these situations what a parent would do if they requested their check on payday and their boss casually dismissed them with, "Sorry, I forgot about you." Wouldn't they panic knowing they needed that money to pay bills and provide for their families? Well, the same is true for daycare providers – they also need to support their families and pay their bills, including paying daycare-related vendors and employees.

Whether your child is in a daycare center or a home daycare, it should be a top priority for parents to remember their daycare payments. After all, without daycare most working parents would not have the freedom to go to work and make a living in the first place.

How would you feel if you owned or operated a business and people continued to utilize your services day after day, but when it came time to pay for those services they would simply say they forgot, then continue to use your services and not pay on time? This happens to daycare providers all the time. We deserve the same common courtesies as anyone else for doing our jobs and we should get paid without having to ask. Remember to make your daycare payments a priority and show your provider the respect they deserve.

No Cell Phone Zone

Let's think about some of the places cell phones might be considered inappropriate to use...at the dinner table, at the movie theater, at a quiet romantic restaurant, during work hours (assuming it's a personal call), during a church service...let's see...where else, oh yeah, your child's daycare!

Day in and day out, we see parents coming in while they are in the middle of a phone call on their cell phone. They barely acknowledge staff with a meek smile, then proceed to "collect" their children, while continuing their phone conversations. There are so many things wrong with this picture, but the biggest one is the little face looking at you, wondering why your phone call is more important, especially since you haven't seen your child all day. Your child, as well as your provider, deserve your full attention every time you walk through those daycare doors.

A parent walked into the lobby one afternoon, on her cell phone, and saw me waving her down. I had something to discuss with her, so I felt no reservations about interrupting her call. She stopped right in front of me, then turned to the person on the phone and said, "the daycare lady needs to talk to me, I gotta go." I stood there thinking, *Really? First of all, I have a name. Second, I'm sorry you were so inconvenienced by having to end your call to discuss your child, which I can guarantee is more important than whatever gossip you were catching up on.* Then no sooner was she done speaking with me, she got right back on her phone as she proceeded to walk in her child's classroom to pick him up.

Now, we realize that occasionally you may have a business call you have to finish up, or maybe you received an important call at the last minute as you came to pick up your child. Be courteous, and finish your phone call outside before coming in to get your child. They really have missed you all day, and I'm sure you missed them too, so make sure your actions reflect your feelings. Before just picking them up and walking out, spend a few minutes with them in their classroom. Ask them to show you what they did that day, and to share with you what they learned. The kids are always excited to share about their day when their parents arrive, but unfortunately, too many times, we see the parents being too busy to notice.

● ● ● ● ●

Many centers will have a "No Cell Phone Zone" sign posted on their front door. And they're not referring to the kids who have phones!

● ● ● ● ●

All's Fair in Love and Donuts

As a home daycare provider, it drives us nuts when parents bring their kids to daycare with special treats or toys just to make drop-off easier. One of the things that daycare providers strive to achieve is for all kids in their care to be treated fairly and equally.

On the way to driving her kids to a home daycare, a mom of three would always stop and buy three chocolate donuts for her children to eat at daycare. She would walk in and set her kids at the table, even though it was not yet breakfast time, and let them eat while she quietly snuck out the door with no fuss. I'm guessing she never considered how terribly unfair this was not only to the other children but also to the provider that had to deal with several upset kids that did not get donuts. The provider mentioned to the mom on several occasions that donuts were not necessary and she would feed her kids the same breakfast the others were given, but each day her kids continued to arrive with their donuts.

One day, when the kids arrived, the provider was waiting with a plastic bag for the donuts. She simply explained to the mom that they would have to put their donuts away and they could eat them on their way home. Mom didn't say much but she put their donuts in the bag while the kids stood and watched, then all three burst into tears. The provider thought this would be the end of the donut situation, but she was wrong. The next day the 3 kids came in carrying a huge white box containing donuts for everyone and wasn't she surprised!

This story didn't exactly go as planned for the daycare provider but at times it's really hard to say things to parents without offending them. If your child really wants something extra, please let them have it before coming to daycare. Your daycare provider will truly appreciate you for it.

Keep It Away

What's worse than a parent who walks in smelling profusely of cigarettes? The parent who's finishing their cigarette in the parking lot of their child's daycare!

When I walked out to my car one day, I saw a parent who was parked smack in front of the building, sitting in their car finishing a cigarette. I remember thinking, *Really? I'm the one feeling embarrassed that you're smoking in front of a daycare center, and you're the one who's smoking!* Just as there are places a cell phone conversation doesn't belong, there are also places where cigarette smoking doesn't belong either, and daycare is one of them! Not only is it a bad example for the little children, but it's also corrupting one of the few innocent places children have left. Let's keep daycare center parking lots free of cigarette fumes and cigarette butts. Your children and your health will thank you for it.

Amongst the daycare providers and staff, there will usually be some smokers. Providers should be very diligent about smoking away from the childcare center premises and be certain there is no remaining smell of smoke on them before they return to work. It becomes a trickier situation when you have a home daycare provider that smokes. When and how often do they give themselves cigarette breaks and who's watching the kids during that time? If you ever smell smoke on your daycare provider or from your children because they were around them, these concerns need to be addressed immediately.

• • • • •

It's very sad when children come in smelling like smoke, or when you see them leave in a car with someone smoking, especially when it's in the wintertime and the window is barely cracked open.

• • • • •

Skinny Jeans Are Not for Everyone!

Another thing that really drives daycare providers nuts is when children do not have extra clothes or underwear and we are left to figure it out. It may not seem like the most important thing to remember but when your child has an accident or gets dirty, they just want the comfort of being changed into their own clothes. If we don't have any, then we need to find something that may not be what your child necessarily wants to wear. In daycare centers, there is often a box of extra clothes donated by parents, but in home daycares, this is usually not the case; instead, the provider may have only her own children's extra clothes to offer, and in some cases nothing extra to offer at all.

A little 4 year old boy had been attending a home daycare for a few years and, as is often the case, the child had outgrown the extra clothes that his parents had originally brought for him which they had forgotten to update. One day the little boy had an accident and the provider realized the only extra clothes he had were a pair of jeans that were two sizes too small. The provider's children were all girls so she chose a pair of grey sweatpants that had a few hearts on one leg and tried to pass them off as "boy" clothes. The little boy was disgusted and refused to wear the "girl" clothes, but his only option soon became his reality. While trying to keep a straight face, his provider squeezed him into the very small jeans and insisted that he looked fine. The little boy seemed uncomfortable at first, but then he went right back to painting a picture and soon forgot about the jeans.

Later that afternoon at pickup time, his dad walked in the door and as soon as he saw his son, he burst out hysterically laughing and said, "Why are you wearing skinny jeans?" Other parents that were also picking up began to laugh as well, causing the little boy to cry. This was not his fault but, as a result, he was not only uncomfortable for hours, but also embarrassed.

We cannot stress enough the importance of remembering to update your child's extra clothes. Even if your child has extra clothes, do they still fit and are they still appropriate for the current season? You might just want to check.

● ● ● ● ●

You know that nightmare some people have where they find themselves caught completely naked and everyone is pointing and laughing? This is probably what your child feels like when they have no extra clothes at daycare!

● ● ● ● ●

 **10.**

A Little Appreciation
Goes A Long Way…

*Do the special people in your life
get the appreciation they deserve?*

A s a parent, you willingly chose to do a job that involves taking care of
your children and all your family's many needs. In addition to this, the
stress on parents that work outside the home, yet are still responsible
for all their family's needs, can push even the most organized and energized
parents to their limits. For all you do in caring for your family, how often do you
actually hear a "thank you" or "good job" from your spouse or kids? Yet you
continue to take care of your home and family,
endlessly washing and folding the same clothes,
shopping for and preparing meal after meal, and
vacuuming and mopping the same crumb-covered
floors, without complaint, because it's what you signed
up to do. You may not even expect to be appreciated

for it anymore, but imagine the joy it would bring you if your spouse walked in every now and then with a small gift of appreciation and thanked you for all your hard work…or your kids gave you a hug and kiss and told you how much they appreciated all you did for them. Knowing you are acknowledged and appreciated for all you do would probably help you do your job with more love and joy instead of grudge and gripe!

When was the last time you thanked your daycare provider for all the hard work they do for you and your children? If you have to stop and think about it, then it's probably been too long. Your provider should be treated with appreciation and respect; after all, they are caring for your most important possession, your child! Find out their birthday, and make them feel as special as they strive to make your child feel every day. Acknowledge them for the little things that tend to go unnoticed as busy days pass us all by. As daycare providers, we can assure you we don't mind the long hours, the busy and chaotic days or even the unpleasant parts of the job, and trust us, there are many. What we do mind is when our hard work and efforts are not appreciated or acknowledged by parents. While you are gone, we work tirelessly to care for your child's every need, to entertain them, to love them and to teach them to love others. We also educate them, direct and re-direct them while we help them learn all of life's little lessons. When our efforts go unnoticed, we are just a little more offended and hurt because we are not dealing with a project or a power point presentation that will help a company to succeed; we are working with your children to help *THEM* succeed. If it weren't for the passion, love and dedication providers feel for the children they care for, they couldn't continue to do their job each and every day with the continuous enthusiasm and smiles the children have come to expect from them. A little appreciation from parents every now and then really would go a long way…

What's the Word?

Through the years, families that have had to move on from my center for different reasons have written the kindest letters to my staff and I. This kind gesture has meant more to us than they could ever imagine. Sometimes, I pull these letters out just to re-read them and get that warm heartfelt feeling all over again. There is so much power in words either spoken or written. Words can make a world of difference to someone about the way they feel about themselves, their job performance, their various roles, and on the overall meaning their life has in this world.

One of the first families that enrolled when I first opened my center over 13 years ago left me this letter upon leaving:

Dear Rita,

My son's last day will be December 27. I have decided that it would be in his best interest if I stay at home and explore the option of becoming a licensed home daycare. I cannot tell you how much I have appreciated the care that he's received from your wonderful daycare. All of your employees are heartfelt and compassionate in their work and it's clear to see that it "trickles" down from its owner—you. God has given you a gift to work with children and it's pleasing to see you motivated to exemplify that gift.

Thank you again and God bless you

With Gratitude,
D.A.

Having never done daycare before, I wasn't sure of my ability to successfully pull this business operation off, but what I *did* know is that I had a passion for loving children and wanted to offer a loving environment in which they could learn, be loved and have fun. After receiving this letter, it confirmed to me that I was on the right track and that when your heart is in something and you're doing it for the right reasons, you will always succeed (it may not always be in a monetarily way). So if you feel you don't have much to give, your words of kindness, appreciation, motivation, inspiration and love are valued above all else.

What's a single word that someone can say to you that would light you up and make you shine? Is it beautiful, charming, sweet, smart, awesome, amazing, irreplaceable, lifesaver, incredible, talented? It's amazing what a single word can do for a person. It's easy to point out what didn't go right, and that's fair, but now and then all we really need to hear is THANK YOU!

Potty Training...Who's Training Who?

Potty training children in daycare can be an extremely challenging thing to do. Children are ready to potty train at different ages and at their own pace but many parents think that if they are ready to be done buying diapers, then their children should be ready to be potty trained!

A little boy was attending a home daycare with about eight other children. He had just turned three but had no interest in using the potty and it was driving his mother crazy. She insisted that she was done buying diapers and he was going to wear underwear and use the potty no matter what! She brought several pairs of underwear and extra clothes in, and insisted *no more diapers!* Now, this may have seemed like a great idea to his mom but the daycare provider ended up having to clean up several huge messes each day, not to mention wasting a lot of time changing a child who was simply not ready. She told the mom every day that he was not ready but the mom insisted her way was best and still no diapers could be worn. At the same time, she would get extremely upset about the soiled clothing that was being sent home every night and often complained about it.

One morning as the mom arrived at daycare with her usual bag of clothing and underwear for her child, she sweetly said to the provider, "I have a present for you." Feeling pleased and happy that the mom had actually noticed her struggle and hard work with her child, the daycare provider excitedly opened the bag the mom had given her and much to her amazement it contained a bottle of stain remover! The mom smiled and said, "I bought this for you so you could get the stains out of my son's underwear before sending them home".

I think in this situation it is fair to assume how the daycare provider felt. Part of a daycare provider's job is to follow the wishes of a parent as much as possible, but parents need to realize the provider is busy with many other things as well. In many cases, providers end up spending more time with kids than their parents do, so what we have to say should really matter and be valued. Also, if parents are not willing to deal with the "dirty work" of being a parent then no one else should have to either. A little "thank you" goes a long way at the end of the day. In fact, it's probably the most important thing a parent can ever say to a provider, and if you feel a gift is necessary, flowers are always nice too!

A Little Text with a Big Message

When we live in a world where people are always rushing and everything is expected to be delivered fast and perfect, we forget how lucky we are...to have our health, our children, our families, a roof over our head, steady income, clean water, and abundance of food and technology at the tip of our fingers. We hardly ever communicate in person anymore – even birthday wishes are done through Facebook or text. It's the world we live in, and we accept it, but what's hard to accept is why it is so much easier to complain than it is to show appreciation. Maybe it's because we feel a sense of entitlement when we are paying for something, and forget that we should still be grateful that someone was willing to do the job and provide the service that we required in the first place...

Daycare providers can receive many texts and emails daily from the families they serve...my child won't be in today, my child needs to be picked up after school, I need a receipt, please save lunch for my child, keep my child up during nap, my child is missing his mittens, how is my child doing, reminder about my child's medication today, Dad will be picking up late today, etc.. In any given day, there can be a slew of messages and reminders coming in from all sorts of directions, and providers are used to this and handle each and every one of these requests.

One afternoon, amidst all the normal chaos, a center director was receiving several texts from a parent concerning her child. Just when she thought the situation was handled, suddenly she received yet another text from that parent. But this time, the text simply said, "By the way, I really appreciate everything all of you do." Such a simple message that meant so much. She stood there and smiled for a minute, then wrote back, "Thanks. We appreciate your appreciation." J

Just a little token of gratitude can make such a big difference in someone's attitude.

Closet Full of Surprises!

It's always nice when someone is shown appreciation and noticed for their dedication and hard work. The few times a year that daycare providers are likely to be shown appreciation from parents are at Christmas time and occasionally on their birthdays. When appreciation is shown on Mother's Day, we know that we have a special place in the hearts of those families and they consider us to be more than just daycare providers.

A home daycare provider was caring for a new family who lived nearby that had a five-year-old boy and a new baby. They were a great family; the provider was happy with the arrangement and adored the kids. One day the parents told the provider that they would be home if she needed to reach them as they took the day off to have a garage sale. After naptime that afternoon the provider decided to take the kids on a walk and let the older kids ride their bikes to the sale.

As the provider walked up to the garage sale with the kids, she immediately noticed a beautiful red armoire. She thought it would be perfect for her home and considered purchasing it, but when she asked about the price, they told her they were selling it for their neighbor and it came with a high price tag. The provider quickly forgot about the cabinet and the kids enjoyed riding bikes and spending time at the sale on such a warm sunny afternoon. Later she returned home with the kids and they went about the rest of their day as usual.

Several weeks went by and Mother's Day rolled around. The provider was enjoying a lazy day with her husband and kids when suddenly there was a knock at her door. When she opened it, she was surprised to see her daycare family standing there with big smiles on their faces. She was also surprised to see a huge trailer backed into her driveway with the beautiful red armoire loaded onto it! "Happy Mother's Day!" they all screamed and the provider's eyes filled with tears. What an honor it was to be celebrated not just by her own children on Mother's Day, but by other's children as well!

There is no greater feeling for a childcare provider than when a family realizes the impact the provider has on their child's life and considers their opinion to be that of a second mom. Being appreciated on Mother's Day is a great honor for childcare providers, and being appreciated and shown how much they mean to a family at any time of the year is priceless!

 **11.**

Eye-Opening Admissions...

It's so easy to jump to the wrong conclusions.

magine receiving a call from your best friend...from jail...and she tells you she's been arrested for a DUI. Your mind would start racing and, despite knowing that she's a very responsible person who would never do such a thing, you might even begin speculating about the details that landed her there. Based on assumptions, you may even be shocked and feel disappointed that she'd ever do such a thing.

Once she begins to explain the events that led to her arrest, they turn out to be much different than what you imagined. She was enjoying a glass of wine while out to dinner with her husband, who did not drink any alcohol. Just shortly after she finished her second glass, her husband became violently ill and she had to drive him home. She was not originally planning on driving, and although she knew she had two glasses of wine, she felt fine and didn't worry about being a threat on the road. When a police officer pulled her over for not fully stopping at a stop sign, he discovered she was just barely over the legal intoxication limit and arrested her.

Now, this incident could've happened to a number of us at some point in our lives. It's easy for others to jump to false conclusions and make assumptions without knowing all the facts. Occasionally, daycare providers with good intentions will also make poor choices when caring for children. They are human, after all, and these poor choices can be due to many factors including juggling too many things at once, not being fully present in the moment, or simply just making a decision or taking action without thinking things through. Either way, there are times when their actions can jeopardize the safety of your child. Seeing the whole picture and understanding the details surrounding each event will help you determine if it truly was an accident or if negligence was involved. After reading these stories, what conclusion would you have jumped to and how would you have reacted before hearing all the relevant details for each event?

Home Alone

A home daycare provider decided to take her group of 8 children to a puppet show at a local park. The kids would typically line up at the front door of her home where their shoes were kept, and when everyone was ready, they would all go out together and get into the van. On this particular day, the children had been playing outside in the backyard and one of the toddlers had left his shoes in the sandbox. The provider asked him to go get his shoes as she busily continued to help the other kids put on sunblock, tie shoes and fill water bottles. Realizing that the show was about to begin, she hurried the kids out the door, into the van and quickly buckled them into their car seats. She pulled out of the driveway and started to drive down the street when she remembered the little boy who had gone to get his shoes. She pulled the van over, and after a quick head count, she realized the child was missing! She immediately panicked and quickly turned around to go get him. That one minute ride back to the house felt like hours!

As she pulled into the driveway, her mind was racing with thoughts of all the horrible things that could happen to a toddler that is left alone. She jumped out of her van and raced to the door. With trembling hands, she fumbled with the keys, unlocked the door, pushed it open and there he was! He looked up at her with a blank expression on his face, shoes still in his hands. She grabbed and hugged him so tightly, and although she was relieved to find he was ok, she knew she would never forget that feeling of terror that coursed through her body when she first discovered he was missing!

Home daycare providers can get so caught up in doing so many things at once (and sometimes in a hurry), that they can forget the most important rule in daycare which is to count heads before and after any transition time and also in between. Again, an incident that started out as a great idea and fun outing for the kids could have turned into tragedy in a second simply because the provider was being pulled in so many different directions at once, and not being mindful and present in all of them. How does your daycare provider handle the pressure of a chaotic day or does the chaos at times get the best of your provider?

Are All Buckles Buckled?

Has this ever happened to you... You're driving along without a care in the world and then turn a sharp corner and whoops! your child's car seat in the back topples forward or off to the side? It's a horrible feeling and it's happened to me more than once with my own children. Suddenly, you're left thinking, *Who the heck undid that seatbelt and why didn't I notice that it was unbuckled?* It's one thing when it happens to you as a parent, and another when it happens to a daycare provider, but either way it does occasionally happen...

A teacher was doing her daily van run which involved picking up only one child from that particular school. When the teacher picked up the little girl, she securely buckled her into the car seat containing a four-harness belt buckle. She then shut the door, got back in, buckled herself up and drove away. As soon as she made the first turn, a loud noise came from the back, followed by the little girl's cry. The teacher, alarmed and unsure of what had just occurred, quickly pulled over to check on the child. When she opened the passenger door, she was shocked to discover the car seat which the little girl was still fastened to, had tipped forward and was now leaning against the back of the front seat. The teacher was confused how this could've happened, then realized that even though she had securely buckled the child into the car seat, she had not double-checked that the car seat was buckled into the car. Someone, perhaps one of the older kids that had been transported in that same van earlier, must have unbuckled it. Thankfully, the little girl was alright with no apparent bumps or bruises but the teacher was shaking badly and close to tears. She safely and securely buckled the child's car seat into place and continued to the daycare center.

After they arrived, she informed the director of what had happened, who double-checked the little girl to make sure she was alright, then called and informed the child's parents. This incident was reported to licensing, who came out to the center to investigate and determine if any negligence was involved.

Licensing determined that maltreatment was involved in this case due to the fact that the teacher did not do all of the required safety checks prior to transporting the child. Since it was a first time offense, the teacher was able to continue working with children, but a secondary occurrence would disqualify her from working with children ever again. The center re-examined and enforced their policies regarding their van drivers and more safety checks were implemented before and after each van run. Unfortunately, the parents of this child were very distraught over the situation, and pulled their child out of the center immediately.

It's important to remember that these events can happen to anyone, but when they happen to a childcare provider, they are looked at with more scrutiny. Our intention for sharing these stories is not only to help make parents more aware of the right questions to ask and the important things to look for in a quality childcare program, but also to remind parents that daycare providers are human, and accidents will still occasionally happen. Depending on the circumstances of an incident, and the severity of what took place, a parent might consider giving the provider and the center another chance.

• • • • •

It's important to always research providers before making your final choice. Other than regular license renewal visits, which can occur anywhere from every 1 to 5 years depending on the state, a licensor will only check on a provider unexpectedly if a complaint has been made against them. All findings and violations occurring from visits are public record and can be viewed online for all licensed providers. When searching for daycare, you can start by googling either the center's name or the home daycare owner's name.

• • • • •

The One Left Behind

One fall day, a class of 18 preschoolers returned from their class field trip to their daycare center just in time for their afternoon nap. When they arrived, one teacher assisted the children out of the van, while the other teacher assisted them into the building. Once they were all inside, the teachers helped them wash up and find their cots, which were already laid out in preparation for their nap. Within ten minutes, all of the children were laying down quietly on their cots. At this time one of the teachers started to count heads to make sure she had all children accounted for. To her surprise and disbelief, she realized a child was missing, which also explained the one cot on the floor that remained empty. Immediately, panic erupted among the teachers as they frantically began to search the bathrooms, and every square inch of the classroom...

Meanwhile, another teacher was returning from her lunch break. As she pulled into the parking lot, she thought she saw a head moving inside one of the daycare vans parked in front of the building. After parking her car, she ran over to the van, only to validate her suspicions that a child was indeed sitting in the van all alone, with the doors locked! As she raced inside to get the van keys, she crossed paths with a frantic preschool teacher on her way out to check the van. At that moment, they realized from the look on each other's faces what had occurred. Both teachers raced over to the van, quickly unlocked the door and found the four year old child, still buckled into his car seat, sitting there confused and alone.

His teacher, breathing a heavy sigh of relief, unbuckled the child with trembling hands and hugged him tightly. The child was fine, but the teacher was sick to her stomach and on the brink of tears. She couldn't believe she had allowed something like this to happen. She had worked at this daycare for nearly six years, and had always prided herself on her commitment to the safety of the children in her care and the quality of her performance she strived so hard to deliver each day. She brought the child in to his classroom and laid him down on his cot. At this time, she realized the severity of what had just occurred and felt the weight of the situation bearing down on her. As she tried to make sense of it all, she was suddenly overcome with the feeling of nausea, and ran to the staff bathroom and vomited. She was excused for the rest of the day as she was in no condition to continue working.

The child's parents were contacted, and this incident was also reported to licensing. This incident haunted this teacher for months and it was an eye-opening example to all the other staff of how failing to follow such a simple, yet crucial procedure, could lead to a catastrophe. Although the teacher did perform a headcount, which is ultimately how she discovered a child was missing, she did the headcount after the children were inside, rather than counting kids as they left the van and again as they entered the building. A sleeping or small child can easily be missed during a quick visual check of a van or bus. In this case, doing a headcount within a ten minute period led the teacher to find the missing child safely, but sometimes even ten minutes can be too long.

There are many tragic stories of children in daycare that have been forgotten and left behind either outside on the playground or in locked vans or buses. In many cases, children were found once providers realized they were missing, but in other instances, providers never noticed a child was missing until that child's parent came to pick them up. Headcounts should be done before children enter the building, as they enter the building, shortly after they are in the classroom, and periodically throughout the day. Many incidents occurred due to the neglect of this very simple but effective procedure.

Ask your daycare provider about their headcount policy and the procedures they follow for keeping track of children leaving and re-entering the building. Familiarize yourself with the routes that children will take from the playground and the parking lot to the classroom, and ask questions about any unclear procedures until you are clear and comfortable with this process. Until you are at ease with the effectiveness of these policies, you may consider calling to check on your child when their class returns from an outing or a field trip. As children come and go throughout the day, providers need to be extremely diligent in their practices of noticing and documenting these changes.

The percentage of children that are overlooked or forgotten is very minor in comparison to the number of children that are accounted for, loved and cared for by providers each day; however, it's understandable that a parent would feel uneasy about their child's safety and well-being while in someone else's care. The number one rule in daycare is that children be supervised and accounted for at all times. There is no fool-proof way to know that your child will always be safe and accounted for but knowing your child attends a daycare that has policies and procedures in place to prevent such incidents from happening in the first place is a good starting point.

The Backup Plan

One of the hardest parts of being a home daycare provider is juggling your home and daycare responsibilities. Providers may miss many personal family events such as school functions, sporting events and teacher conferences due to

their daycare responsibilities, but nothing is worse than when parents change plans at the last minute and providers find themselves in situations where tough decisions must be made.

A daycare provider was placed in a tough predicament when a parent called at the last minute to say that she would be late picking up her kids that day. The provider explained to this parent that since she had just recently moved to the area, she didn't have anyone else to help pick up her own children from school, and she also did not have enough room in her car for all the kids to safely fit. The parent replied that there was nothing she could do about it, but that she would come as soon as possible. After trying unsuccessfully to figure out what to do, the provider made the decision to put all the daycare kids in her available car seats, while buckling her own two children together in one seat for the short ride home.

On the way home, after picking up the kids, the provider failed to stop completely at a stop sign and was pulled over by the police. All the kids were taken out of her car, and driven by the police to the police station to wait for their parents to pick them up. The children were scared, and the parents that were called were only told that the daycare provider had endangered their children. She had made a split second decision with few options to consider that turned into one of the worst experiences of her life.

Parents need to consider the consequences of their actions and the position of the daycare provider when they change plans at the last minute or pick their children up late. Your daycare may be able to accommodate your needs most of the time, but you also need to understand that you may be leaving your provider, and consequently your child, in a bad situation where options are limited and an undesirable ending is a possibility.

12.

Behind Closed Doors

What really happens when no one is watching?

Picture this: You are enjoying a nice evening out to dinner with a group of friends at one of your favorite restaurants. As you settle into the plush cherry-colored leather booth, you relax with a glass of fine wine, and enjoy good conversation with friends with classical music playing softly in the background. After a long work week, it really doesn't get much better than this. Behind the kitchen's closed doors, however, there is a different scenario playing out… Both chefs called in sick that night, so the understaffed kitchen crew is scrambling around doing their best to grill steaks and prepare pleasant-looking dinner plates. In all this chaos, your $30 steak happens to fall to the floor and, without giving it much thought, the cook quickly picks it up and throws it on the grill. No harm done, he thinks, since the fire will burn off any dirt and germs anyway, and the customer will be none the wiser. As predicted, you are none the wiser as you enjoy your meal and finish every last bite of the steak you paid for with your hard-earned money.

A steak is one thing, but when it comes to your child, how do you really know what occurs throughout the day before they are served to you at pickup time with a fresh clean face, big smile and a daily report detailing the day's events? Unfortunately, not everyone who chooses to work with children has their hearts and intentions in the right place, so what you see at the end of the day may not always represent a complete picture of what actually happened that day. Most home daycare providers (often operating for 12 hours a day) are probably also tending to the needs of *their* families and homes during this time. In daycare centers, where there are usually a few staff members working together in each classroom, there can be more socializing and personal cellular phone use at times than care-giving. Knowing the right questions to ask, and the red flags to look for, will help reveal a more accurate picture of what might really be going on behind closed doors.

Singing in the Rain

For over a year, my friend's two girls attended a small home daycare. They were very happy there and loved their daycare provider. The provider had three daughters of her own and all of the girls were best friends. My friend admits that she never really asked for details about daycare since her girls would talk non-stop about all the fun they would have and new things they would learn each day. She also didn't give much thought to what the provider would do all day, other than to assume she was doing her job. Whereas my friend sometimes felt overwhelmed caring for just her two children at home, her provider was caring for six children! She would often jokingly say, "I wonder if she ever has time to sit down?"

One morning my friend called me in tears to say that something horrible had happened at daycare and she wasn't sure what to do. She explained that after arriving at work, she realized she had forgotten to pay the daycare provider, so she returned during her morning break to take care of it. When she walked into the house, she could see the four girls watching TV together on the couch while two smaller children were playing together nearby. What she didn't see was the daycare provider. Confused, she started to look around and asked the kids where she was. They replied that she was in the shower but… *that couldn't be true, could it?* She walked down the hall towards the bathroom and could hear singing coming from the running shower! Completely shocked, she knocked on the door. The daycare provider came out a few minutes later acting as if nothing were wrong. She explained that every morning after breakfast, the kids would watch TV while she took a shower and got ready for the day. My friend understood that this was the provider's home but she had never considered the idea that the provider would be tending to personal things during daycare hours. She left that day in tears with the girls, feeling very much like she had been deceived. She had trusted this woman and was paying her good money to watch her girls, but now she was left wondering if this sort of thing was a common occurrence and actually happened in other home daycares.

Dropping in from time to time at your home daycare is always a good idea. Don't worry about whether or not you will be disturbing your provider or if your child might get upset. Rather, worry about what you might miss if you don't. Just because home daycare providers are at home does not mean that they should be doing personal or household chores during the time they are operating a childcare business. You are paying for your child to be cared for and supervised while you are at work. You are not paying your daycare provider to shower, do her laundry or talk on the phone. Occasionally, all home daycare providers may take advantage of naptime to start dinner for their own families or to pay a few bills; after all, they are usually operating for 12 hours a day and everyone receives some sort of break during working hours. However, if a provider's multi-tasking with personal duties jeopardizes your child's safety, it becomes a problem, and sometimes different arrangements must be made. Don't assume that these things never happen in your child's home daycare; pop in one day unannounced and see for yourself.

Social Hour

Many years ago I was working as a director at a busy daycare center. One issue that seemed to come up repeatedly was that staff would often socialize with each other while working in the same classroom. We addressed this issue time and time again but this behavior would still reoccur.

Our toddler room was a very busy place. We had 21 toddlers with three providers and most of the kids were just turning two. Constant supervision was a must with so many young children and turning your back for even a second could result in disaster. One afternoon, the toddlers were outside on the playground which was surrounded by a large wooden fence with a gate that led out to the parking lot. The teachers were supposed to separate outside so that the entire playground was being monitored and all of the kids would be safe. On this particular day, the conversation must have been especially good because all three of the teachers were sitting on a large wooden climber together having "social time" while three toddlers opened the gate and were heading out into the busy parking lot, completely unseen.

I came out to check on numbers and immediately saw the open gate and the three ignorant staff members. They realized quickly what had happened and ran to the gate to get the three children. Luckily the children hadn't gotten very far, but if I hadn't come out right then, this event could have easily ended in tragedy. The three teachers were put on probation and separated from each other in different classrooms and licensing as well as the children's parents were informed about this unfortunate incident. Even after this shocking event and this huge wake-up call for the teachers, I bet things like this still happen in daycares across the country every single day. Teachers will chat with one another and lose sight of the job they are supposed to be doing. It takes a special kind of person to stay engaged and present in what the children are doing all day and to not get distracted by text messages, phone calls or the latest juicy gossip.

Working in a daycare center requires staff to have a certain dedication and diligence to the job that they are choosing to do every day. Excuses in this profession come at the expense of a child's safety and well-being and having a bad day could result in many children having a bad day as well. It's a job that requires staff to bring their "A game" every day and to never fall short of the high expectations required of them. This job is not for everyone and thinking that playing with kids all day sounds like a fun and easy career choice could quite possibly be the biggest misconception someone considering becoming a provider could ever make!

Where Did Everyone Go?

It's very common for childcare workers to call in sick, and due to the amount of illness and germs they are exposed to, it probably happens more frequently than in most professions. Most centers have substitute teachers or agencies they can call when backup is needed but there will always be those days when too many staff members are unable to come in and, regardless of backup options, classrooms can end up running over ratio. This jeopardizes the quality and safety of the children's care. One center's director experienced such a day, which turned out to be one of the craziest days in her daycare career!

This director recalls returning to work on her first day after a restful maternity leave, completely unprepared for what she was about to encounter. That morning, one of the teachers had a scheduled day off and two other teachers had called in sick. A fourth teacher's child had gotten sick so she had to leave an hour after she arrived, and the cook had received an emergency phone call and left right after breakfast, leaving behind a sink full of dirty dishes and lunch still to be made. All the backup substitutes had been called but, unfortunately, none were unavailable.

When she arrived, hoping to slowly ease back into her job, she was thrown into a tornado of chaos and didn't know where to start first. Two of the teachers with early opening shifts were waiting for someone to break them, and every room was running over ratio. She started in the infant room, which seemed to be the calmest at the time. She needed a moment to figure out the best plan for the day, but no matter how she figured it, they would be short-staffed and rooms would have to run over ratio!

As her day continued, giving one break after another and trying to get lunch together, she didn't get a chance to take her own needs into consideration and realized a new issue had formed. She had planned to return to work without her baby at first, who was being cared for by a close relative, and to pump several times a day to be able to continue breastfeeding. In all of the chaos and craziness, she had forgotten to take time to pump and had now become fully engorged and was feeling extremely uncomfortable. Nevertheless, there was nothing she could do at that point, so she worked through the pain!

Everyone did their best that day to meet the demands of the job while keeping classrooms under control and the children safe and supervised. The director's biggest fear that day wasn't that licensing could make a surprise visit and cite the center for operating understaffed or that a parent might notice how there were more children than required caregivers; her biggest fear was that an accident might occur due to being understaffed or that a child's needs might not be properly met due to the circumstances of the day. Accidents will occasionally happen that are unpreventable, but if an accident happened on a day like that, it would have seemed inexcusable. Children's safety and well-being should always come first and foremost, in daycare as well as at home. So everyone stepped up that day and gave their all to ensure that happened.

Later that afternoon, rooms were finally back in proper ratio as children began to leave. The madness was over and everyone was relieved and grateful that all the children made it through the day unharmed. The teachers all pulled through a difficult day, with a little less sanity to show for it, and it's times like these it's so important to have such dedicated teachers willing to put in that extra effort!

In this example, it was clearly a crazy and stressful day that no one would want to relive. Unfortunately, when home providers take in more children than they are allowed, or when centers do not have enough staff and backup to meet staff-to-child ratio requirements, days like these become a recurring problem. Every center should have a backup plan for staff absences but sometimes even the backup plan can't be relied upon. Like any business place, daycare centers can have crazy, out-of-control days, but they should be few and far between. Pay attention to your child's classroom and make sure the center is consistently operating within ratio. You may ask to see a home provider's license to verify how many children of each age group they are allowed to have. Ultimately, your child's safety and well-being is dependent on how well and appropriately providers are operating.

What's in the "Pot"?

In a nice suburban neighborhood on a tree-lined street with pretty houses and beautifully manicured lawns, one home had a sign out front advertising home daycare services. If what you see on the outside is a fair indication of the type of childcare program being offered on the inside, you would have no worries and no reason to look any further. In reality, what was behind this home's impressive doors was not a pretty picture at all.

A couple dropped their toddler off at a home daycare, as they had done many times before, and went off to work. At the end of their workday, they picked up their daughter and headed home to start dinner. Within the next few hours, their daughter became very lethargic and didn't look or feel well. They decided to take her into the emergency room. Upon assessing her condition, the doctor decided they needed to draw her blood to get a proper diagnosis. After analyzing the blood tests, the doctor delivered the shocking news to the anxious parents: the results showed traces of marijuana in the child's system. The parents were in complete, utter shock and disbelief and couldn't wrap their heads around what they had just been told. They realized the only place their daughter had been that day was at daycare. The hospital reported this incident, as required, to the authorities.

The following day, authorities showed up at the home daycare to investigate and what they found was unbelievable! After completing a thorough search of the home, they found the facility smelling strongly of urine and they found mouse droppings in areas where the kids would play. There were dirty dishes piled up in the kitchen sink and sharp knives within the children's reach. The toilets didn't work, the electricity had been shut off and, last but not least, a bong and other drug paraphernalia were found out in the open.

The most ironic part of this story is that while this search was being conducted, eight families tried to drop their children off at this daycare and were turned away by authorities. When these families were informed of the findings, they were confused, to say the least, and many couldn't believe what they were hearing. They were unaware of, and had never seen, any of these conditions. When neighbors were interviewed, they stated they weren't surprised about what had been found. They claimed they would see children constantly crying at the windows while the provider would be outside on her cell phone.

The home daycare facility was deemed unlivable and was shut down immediately and condemned by officials. It leaves you wondering how parents could drop off their children at such a place.

As a parent, you're probably wondering how something like this can happen without your knowledge. Believe it or not it's easier than you think to make something appear to be different than it actually is. If your child attends a home daycare, does the provider always greet you in one certain area of the home so that you have no chance to see any other parts of the house? You may think this is a convenience and it just may be, but it can also be a blazing red flag. Is it possible that there is something your provider just doesn't want you to see? Initially you may have been shown the entire house and everything checked out just fine, but if your child is spending time in a home, then you need to be aware of what's in the home at all times. It's very disturbing as well as disheartening that this incident could occur, but at the same time it's a great eye-opener for parents to realize they need to make a conscious effort and be more aware of what is going on behind closed doors at their child's daycare.

The only way you may know what is truly going on behind closed doors is to open those doors yourself and take a peek. If your child is always ready and waiting for you in one certain area of your provider's home, be suspicious. The provider in the above story specifically would discourage parents from going into the other rooms in her home, for good reason, and yet parents obliged without any suspicions! You should feel completely comfortable to walk into the areas where the children eat, play, sleep, and do activities anytime you like. Evidence of what the child has done all day, like artwork and activities, should be present in these areas. Occasionally, ask to use the bathroom to see what condition it is in. Is their soap at the sink and is the bathroom clean? Ask if you can help yourself to a glass of water in the kitchen. If these things seem uncomfortable to you, then you are in the wrong place. Make unannounced visits every so often. This will show you a more accurate picture of what's really going on behind those closed doors, and hopefully keep unwelcome surprises or shocking incidents from occurring.

• • • • •

An assistant was hired at a center and after working a few days, her co-workers complained to the director that she smelled like marijuana. She had passed her background check and the director hadn't noticed or smelled anything unusual about her. The next afternoon, right after the assistant returned from her lunch break, the director called her into the office. At that point, she clearly picked up the smell of marijuana coming from the assistant's clothes and also noticed her eyes were completely bloodshot! Shocked, the director looked at her and asked, "Have you been smoking marijuana?" The assistant looked back at the director with a straight face and bloodshot eyes and said, "No. I would never do such a thing." She was fired on the spot! When it comes to people that want to work in childcare, like most other professions, know that they come in all kinds!

• • • • •

Section III:

The Child

Childhood is a once-in-a-lifetime experience that should be celebrated each day…

When you think back to your childhood, what's the first thing you remember? One thing that stands out for many is the simplicity and innocence of our young lives. Life was easy and our problems few. What we didn't realize was how hard it was to be the parent. Now that we are in the parental role, we have the difficult job of trying to make all the right decisions for our children in hopes of raising them to be the best individuals possible.

When asked to state in one word what your children mean to you, many would quickly say "everything". We give "everything" we have, including our hearts and souls, to our children in hopes of having it come back to us someday in the form of their success, confidence and love. We do "everything" in our power to control and monitor their influences, guide them down the right paths and meet their every need. We sacrifice "everything" to ensure their safety and well-being, and challenge "everything" that gets in their way or tries to harm them. We are their protectors, providers, best friends and sometimes their worst enemies. They come into our lives for such a short time, shake things up and, before you know it, they leave to make their own mark on the world. Surrounding your child with the right caregivers at a young age, is one of the most important investments you will ever make in your child's life.

It really does take a village to raise a child and our job as parents is to create that village by filling it with loving, trustworthy and positive role models. Their first caregivers will help them to become strong, confident individuals with strong foundations to stand on through life's rough patches and storms. Childhood goes by in the blink of an eye and we can only make decisions for them for a short time, so we need to choose wisely while we can.

✚13.

You Just Might be Surprised...

Life's little surprises are usually the best!

Everyone loves a surprise, but few are as heartwarming as surprises that involve children. When the day arrives for your child to start daycare, you may be nervous and unsure about how your child will do. What you may not expect is how well your child ends up embracing this experience.

Certain parents feel if they place their children in daycare, their children will end up scarred in some way. It is usually these same kids that tend to thrive and enjoy the experience the most. Letting your kids go and trusting that you are leaving them in good hands will show you how strong and adaptable they really are, and you just might learn a thing or two about them in the process. Parents may leave a crying child at the door, and feel guilty and sad all day long, but their children, on the other hand, may be busy playing five minutes later without a care in the world!

Remember, daycare is a little world custom made for children that's full of people and things their own size. Just because you cannot be with your child, doesn't mean that they are at a disadvantage. Instead of feeling guilty, parents should feel good about giving their children the opportunity to learn and socialize at such a young age. The following stories will open your eyes to just what an advantage these kids really do have. You just might be surprised how ready your child is to be a part of this world!

Daycare Dilemma...

Daycare providers are used to getting calls from nervous parents that have no idea what to ask or first steps to take. These parents usually have the enthusiasm of a person calling the dentist to schedule a root canal. Typically, though, after a few minutes of guidance and a little reassurance, they calm down and realize that their kids are not going off to boot camp, just daycare. Occasionally, we will get a call from a parent who is resentful about having to put their child in daycare because they have to start working and have no choice. These are the interesting calls…

A mom called a home daycare provider and asked if she could enroll her two-year-old boy, but just for a week or two. Knowing that kids sometimes need short-term care for different reasons, the daycare provider said yes, then inquired about this parent's situation. The mom was silent on the other end for a little while, then she started to cry! Confused by this, the provider asked the mom what was wrong. The mom sadly replied that she didn't work or need to put her child in daycare but her husband felt their child needed time with other kids. The provider then asked why she needed only two weeks of care, and the mom said she agreed with her husband to a two-week trial period. After that time, if the child was not happy, then she would not continue using daycare. The provider hesitantly agreed to meet with the family and they set up an interview for the following day.

The next day arrived and the family was almost an hour late for their appointment. They all seemed pretty miserable when they arrived and the provider assumed correctly that the daycare debate was continuing. As they began to discuss their child, it was quickly apparent that mom and dad were on two very different pages. Mom felt daycare was not only unnecessary, but that children under five should be at home with their families. Dad felt the boy needed exposure to other children and to begin learning skills needed for school readiness. During this debate, the one thing that surprised the provider was the child! He had very independently chosen a toy train from a tall shelf of buckets and was sitting on a carpet nearby playing happily.

Well, after much consideration, the parents decided to give daycare a try, though Mom was still very much against it, and the following Monday morning both parents showed up to drop their child off. Although the provider was nervous about how the day would go, she assured the parents that everything would be fine, so they finally left. Hesitantly, the provider introduced the child to the other kids and without so much as a tear, he walked over and chose the same train from the shelf and began to play without a second thought. The rest of the day went smoothly as the child played, ate his meals, had his diapers changed and took a nap. He didn't speak much to the other kids but the fact that he was doing so well for the first day, away from Mom, was all that mattered.

Later that afternoon, after several phone calls, Mom came through the door looking like she had been crying all day and stopped in her tracks when she saw her son. He was sitting at a small table with three other kids eating animal crackers and looking quite content. She had obviously expected the worst and now was pleasantly surprised. The provider explained to his mom that the child had indeed had a great day and the days that followed were even better. This boy loved coming to daycare, he made friends, learned new things each day and, three years later, he is still attending the same daycare and still loving it.

Obviously in this situation, Mom was not ready to let her child go, which was no surprise since no mom ever is. As parents, it's extremely scary to send our kids into new situations for fear that they won't be able to handle themselves without us, but in reality, it's the best thing we can do for them. Kids are born eager to learn, grow, develop, and make friends and they thrive when they are placed in loving, stimulating environments. Parents often find themselves surprised at how well their children react to the daycare environment.

I Need Holding

A common concern among parents of infants is whether or not their babies will get enough attention and be held enough – especially for babies that are held a lot at home.

A parent once called to get information about my center and she surprised me with a very odd question. She asked if we would enroll a baby that was held a lot at home. I didn't understand her question until she explained that the infant teacher at the last center she toured told her she needed to stop holding her baby so much so he would get used to what it would be like in daycare. I was surprised to hear this, and could tell she was too. She went on to tell me that she had even double-checked with her baby's pediatrician if holding her baby too much would be harmful in any way. Of course the doctor had assured her that no baby could be "spoiled" just by being held too much. It really bothered me that someone, especially in the childcare field, would say something so ridiculous and make a parent question their loving actions. I shared my own experience with her and explained how I couldn't hold my children enough when they were babies. I got really good at doing everything with one arm, as I held them in the other. I never wanted to put them down, and I would actually get sad when they fell asleep, knowing I should lay them down instead of hauling them around as I did chores.

I shared with her a story of another parent who, prior to enrolling, also had similar concerns about her baby being held enough…

This mother already had her older children in our care for several years, but when it came time to enroll her newborn baby, she was very nervous about the care and attention he would receive. I explained to her how staff always did their best to hold all the babies as much as they could. In addition, if they needed an extra hand, between myself, the assistant director and office assistant, one or more of us were almost always available to help. (And we loved holding babies!) I also told her I was certain her baby would quickly adjust to his new environment, and with so much constant activity and stimulation in the classroom, he probably wouldn't need to be held as much as he was at home anyway. Nevertheless, she remained concerned and warned that she would be calling often to check on him.

On the child's first day, I sat and had a little chat with our new two-month-old student. As I spoke to him and let him know we would hold him as much as possible but he would have to work with us in order to have a successful experience, he stared at me with wide-eyed curiosity. I think I even saw a tiny smile appear on his cute little face. I then called his mom and told her about our little chat; she was amused and thanked me for the update.

As expected, he did cry a bit more during his first couple weeks, but by the third week, he had settled into his new environment and hardly ever cried. He had many new things to look at, a lot of stimulation from music playing and teachers singing, and plenty of new friends to socialize with. He turned out to be one of the happiest and most content babies in the room! His mother was both surprised and relieved at how well her son had adjusted in such a short period of time…but that didn't stop him from still wanting to be held a lot at home!

No one should ever tell parents that they hold their baby too much; on the contrary, we could all use more "downtime" just holding and cuddling our children (if they let us.) Once they turn three, they usually don't care to be cuddled as much, so we have to get it all in while we can. Babies that are held often usually end up feeling more secure as a result.

It's obviously not possible for babies to be held in daycare as much as they are at home, or immediately each time they cry. Centers without extra staff available cannot always tend to a crying baby immediately; regardless, all crying babies should be cared for within a reasonable amount of time. The infant room can be the most stressful to handle without extra support, so find out how your daycare handles this issue. At the end of the day, as long as children are surrounded by loving, caring individuals that strive to give as much attention and affection as possible, they will receive all the benefits of a positive daycare experience.

One Size Doesn't Fit All...

Parents need to consider many factors when trying to find the perfect daycare fit for their child. Will the location fit into their commute? Will the tuition fit into their budget? While searching for the perfect fit, do parents consider if their child will be a good fit for that daycare environment?

At two years old, a very active little boy was enrolled in a home daycare down the street from his house. His mom had warned the provider upon enrolling him that he was a very busy child and always on the go! She also mentioned that he had given up naps a year earlier and his last home daycare provider had a hard time keeping up with him. Even though the daycare provider was used to caring for active kids, this information did make her a bit nervous; nevertheless, she happily accepted the adorable child and welcomed him into her daycare. Since she always kept her daycare kids very busy with daily walks to the park, swimming lessons in the summer and a large play set and trampoline in her backyard, she was fairly certain he would do just fine.

A few weeks went by and this little boy quickly became everyone's best friend. He was happy, extremely verbal and, like his mom had warned, always operating at full speed. The provider couldn't help but love the charming toddler but quickly learned that he created many safety hazards she wasn't prepared for. He would take off at full speed across an open field while they were playing at the park. He would open doors and try to run into the street while they were home. And he would fearlessly perform dangerous stunts while playing on outdoor equipment or the trampoline. The provider soon felt helpless and out of control. If the child wasn't directly next to her, she would fear he may run away, and she would have to leave the other children, including babies, unattended while she chased after him. As much as she hated to let this child go, she knew that a small home daycare with kids of many ages was not the right place for him. He needed a daycare center where he would be in a classroom with other kids his age, and a lot of constant activity and stimulation. He also needed to be in a daycare where more than one caregiver was available to care for the group. The provided arranged a meeting with the child's parents and, a week later, the provider sadly said goodbye to him.

The silver lining to this cloud is that after several weeks the mom sent the provider a thank you card saying the child was doing great in his new daycare center. He had settled in quickly, made new friends, and she was no longer worried about his safety or the safety of others in the daycare. You might just be surprised to find out that when problems arise at daycare, it might have more to do with the environment than the child. One environment really doesn't suit all when it comes to daycare, just as one workplace doesn't suit the personality of every adult. This sweet little boy's behavior was considered to be a problem and he was being asked to leave home daycares, but in reality, he was just in a setting that couldn't accommodate his high-energy. The checklist is long when trying to find the perfect fit, but make sure matching your child's personality to the environment is at the top of that list.

Giving it Time

During the initial start at a new daycare, drop-offs can often be more difficult, and sometimes a child can take longer to adjust than expected. Parents may end up leaving their crying children behind, only to then worry about them for the rest of the day. It is especially difficult for children that begin daycare for the first time at three or four years of age. They tend to have a much harder time getting accustomed to new caregivers as well as being in a new environment surrounded by many children.

A little boy started daycare a month shy of turning three. Since one of his parents had always stayed home, the child hadn't needed daycare, but his parents felt it was time he got some socialization and learning, and enrolled him part-time at a center. This child was also an only child, which in many cases can make it that much more difficult to adjust to an environment where attention from adults can spread thin, and toys need to be shared.

During his first few weeks in daycare, the child cried every time he was dropped off and, for a while, after his parents would leave. He would also hold onto his security blanket throughout the day, sucked his thumb often and didn't eat well at mealtimes. Since his parents were concerned about the difficulty he was having, they would often call to check on him. His teachers admitted that he was having a difficult time but they also expressed their optimism of his eventually doing better, reassuring the parents that different children adjusted at different paces. His parents remained concerned and apprehensive whether the day would ever come when the teachers would report that their son had finally adjusted and was doing well.

Somewhere into the third month, the child stopped using his blanket as much but still occasionally sucked his thumb. Things continued to progress slowly and, in time, he gradually began to socialize and interact with the other children. Unfortunately, he would still get very upset during drop-offs and continued to not eat much at mealtimes. These two issues deeply concerned his parents, and they began doubting the decision they had made to place their child in daycare.

One day, his mom contacted the center's director about her concerns. She wasn't sure if her son should continue to attend, and wondered if he might do better in a smaller daycare setting, with less children. Aware of the progress this child had made, the director was surprised at the mom's hesitation to continue. She thought the mom was also aware of his progress, but soon realized she wasn't witness to her child's experiences at daycare as the teachers were. The director tried to encourage her with many examples of progress that she and the teachers had seen over the course of the past few months which proved that her child was in fact enjoying this experience more than he let on: He was participating in activities and had made some good friends, which had really helped the child come out of his shell. After hearing this information, the mom felt much better and decided to keep him enrolled.

A few more months went by and the child had really transformed by this point. He had begun to look forward to coming to daycare each day and was enjoying all that it had to offer. One evening, when his mom came to pick him up, he began crying immediately at the sight of her. She and her teachers shared a worried look, unsure of what set him off. Then the child yelled out to his mom, "I don't want to go yet!" As surprised and overjoyed as his mom was, the staff was even more ecstatic. They took great pride in this child's breakthroughs, knowing they played a big part in his accomplishments. To this day, when he gets upset because it's time to leave, his mom and teacher share a look that says, *Is this the same child that was struggling to adjust only a few months ago?*

Different children may do better in different size groups but, ultimately, it's the environment and the caregiver's encouragement that will determine a child's success in daycare. This particular case showed how it could take a lot longer than usual for some children to adjust, but that any child can eventually find happiness in a setting where he feels loved, secure and comfortable. Parents might just be surprised how well their children can adapt and flourish when given some time.

● ● ● ● ●

A parent whose child was new to daycare was having a hard time believing teachers that her toddler would cry for only five minutes after she left each morning. After being dropped off, he would throw such a fit, sometimes even throwing himself onto the floor, that it was making her miserable to leave him like that. One morning, her child's teacher suggested she wait outside the classroom for five minutes, then check on him again. She did this and, sure enough, when she peeked in, he had not only stopped crying, but he was playing too! So happy and relieved to see this, she continued to watch him probably longer than she should have, and suddenly he caught a glimpse of her and ran back to the door again and began crying again! It's amazing how fast they can squeeze those tears out! She knew at that point he was just fine, and quickly got over the guilt of leaving her crying son at the door each morning.

● ● ● ● ●

14.

It's the Little Things That Matter Most…

Are you paying attention to the little things that can mean so much?

It's not until you plan your first outing with your new baby that you suddenly realize just how much you need to pack to walk out the door! If you have ever stepped out with your baby and forgot to pack all the necessities into the overflowing diaper bag which now doubles as your designer purse, you may have found yourself in some very loud, messy and uncomfortable situations. The same applies at daycare, so ensuring that your child is fully prepared and has everything needed is key to a successful experience.

Somewhere in between rushing out the door each morning and trying to make it to work on time, we are attempting to drop our children off at daycare. In the everyday hustle and bustle of life, it's easy to get distracted and sometimes disconnect from the reality that our kids are facing at daycare.

We may tend to think that if we make it to daycare on time, without any major meltdowns or setbacks, then our part is done and we can turn our focus to our "second job" for the rest of the day. While this may be true for the most part, we still need to ensure that our children's needs are always being met, and although we have the best of intentions, and want our kids to be successful, these are things that can easily get overlooked.

Stop for a second and consider what your child may need in order to have a successful day. How are they feeling and have they rested well the night before? (We all know what a day at the office is like when you're sick or tired; the same can be true for a child at daycare.) Are you staying connected to them emotionally and celebrating with them the small victories that daycare offers? Do they have extra clothes (weather-appropriate), enough diapers, and maybe that favorite blanket that gets them through the day? Have you taken the extra time to spend a few minutes in their classroom and find out what's important to them and who their best friends are? Whether it's paying attention to their pudding painting (which you may find sticky and gross) or ensuring they have all they need, it's these little things that can mean so much to your child and can make such a difference to their overall daycare experience.

• • • • •

Once, when my 3rd child was a toddler, I was visiting family in California, and we were all out to a restaurant for dinner. After the foul smell in my daughter's diaper spoiled my appetite, I took her to the restroom to change her, only to find I didn't resupply her diaper bag with more diapers. I was completely out, so my sister returned with several cloth dinner napkins which we used as a makeshift diaper! It was a struggle to make it work and, needless to say, it was an uncomfortable situation for the both of us. You'd think by the 3rd one, I would have known better!

• • • • •

Baby Blues

A daycare provider was caring for a baby born several weeks prematurely. One morning, as the baby's mom was dropping him off, the provider noticed that his breathing sounded labored and his color didn't look quite right. When the provider questioned the mom, she replied that the baby had a cold but he had slept well and seemed fine to her. The provider was hesitant yet took the baby, and within an hour, the baby was doing much worse. His breathing was becoming more labored and his lips began to appear rather blue. The provider became scared and immediately tried to call his mom and dad at work but couldn't reach either of them. She found out that his dad was home sick, but was unsuccessful reaching him there either. She was becoming increasingly nervous and began calling the emergency contacts listed for the baby, all to no avail. She was just about to pack up the baby and head to the hospital, when the child's father finally called back.

The child's father explained to the provider that he was not feeling well and had stayed home to rest. He said the baby had been up most of the night with a cough but they had given him Tylenol that morning and thought he would be OK. The provider was very upset to learn this new information, and wondered why Dad didn't keep the baby home with him. She made it very clear to Dad that if he wasn't at her house in ten minutes, she would call an ambulance. He said he would come right away, which he did. Later that afternoon, when they called from the hospital, the provider's fears were confirmed. The child had a severe respiratory virus and needed to spend the next nine days in the hospital in intensive care. The doctors had informed the parents that if the child had gone to sleep at the daycare provider's house, he could have died.

This event could have ended in tragedy. Luckily, the daycare provider was a mom with many years' experience and was well aware of the warning signs that indicated something was seriously wrong. A fully qualified but less experienced provider might have thought the baby just had a cold and may not have monitored him as closely. This is what parents need to realize when they choose to bring sick children to daycare. Not only are their children going to infect all of the other healthy children but they may also end up feeling miserable all day whether you give them Tylenol or not. If you, as a parent, wouldn't want to spend a day at the office tired or sick, why would you bring your child to daycare in such a state? Remember, even though they are little, a child's feelings still do matter. So make the wise decision of keeping the little ones home when necessary.

Messy Madness

Two brothers were attending a home daycare for the summer and they loved nothing more than to get dirty. They loved painting activities, mud pie baking, and especially playing with shaving cream. They would spend hours creating things and often go through several sheets of paper before they were fully satisfied with their creations. One day, the daycare provider taped huge pieces of paper to the floor and let the kids use straws to blow paint around to make colorful, creative designs. The boys loved every minute of this activity and at the end of the day they even asked if they could do another painting before their mom picked them up, which the provider happily agreed to.

About half an hour later, their mom pulled up and the boys were very happy to see her. They grabbed their paintings off the table, where they were almost done drying, and ran to the door where their mom had just walked in. They excitedly began to show her their paintings but instead of her praising them and being thrilled with their work, she seemed angry and screamed at them to keep the messy wet paint away from her. The daycare provider stepped in and informed the mom that it was washable paint and that she would put the paintings in a bag for the boys to carry home. The mom screamed, "No way is that mess coming in my car!" and ordered the boys to throw the paintings in a nearby garbage can. The boys looked absolutely heartbroken and close to tears as they walked over to the garbage can and threw their paintings inside. Silently, the three of them walked out the door. The provider now clearly understood why the boys loved to get messy so much at daycare, because they were never allowed to do that at home. The provider walked over to the garbage can and carefully pulled out both paintings which she then taped to the wall in her kitchen for everyone to see. The boys were overjoyed in the morning to see that their masterpieces were important to someone! So...messy or not, kids should have a place to be kids.

Daycare is a place where kids should feel free to learn new things, discover new ideas, have fun making creative messes, and just be themselves. They spend a lot of time and take a lot of pride in the things they do in daycare and school, so when parents don't even take the time to acknowledge these things, it can make them feel their accomplishments are not important. Throwing away school projects and emptying overflowing backpacks may seem like just another chore for parents to do, but to the children it means something completely different. Of course, not everything they create can be saved, but a moment of acknowledgment from parents can bring children immense joy. Big messy, drippy, paintings proudly displayed on your kitchen wall may not be your idea of décor, but to your child, it will be the best wall in the house, and that's all that really matters!

Brrrrrrr...

It was snowing out...light and fluffy snow perfect for making a snowman...

One morning in a busy daycare center, after the children had completed their morning activities and cleaned up, they were excited to hear it was warm enough for them to finally play outside. They'd been stuck indoors for several weeks due to freezing weather. (State regulations vary but in Minnesota, kids can be outside if it's above 20 to 30 degrees without wind chill.) They prepared to get their snow gear on, grabbing excitedly for jackets, hats and gloves, then they ran over to the area where boots and snow pants were stored to finish getting ready. Teachers eagerly assisted the children with getting their gear on, while children scrambled to find missing gloves and hats. (When getting ready to play outside in snowy weather, it can often take more time to get ready than the actual time they end up playing outside.)

It never fails though, that every winter season, some children will have soft mittens instead of waterproof snow gloves, and others will be without snow pants or boots. Sure enough, that day was not unlike any other, and several children did not have what they needed to be properly protected from the cold and snow. After posting many signs on the front door, as well as personally reminding parents to bring their children's snow gear, some parents still neglected to bring the necessary items for outside playtime. The teachers glanced at each other with a long sigh, thinking, *Here we go again...*

The teachers did what they could with what they had at that point. One teacher looked through the extra bucket of unclaimed items and put a few sets of mittens together, and eventually everyone was ready to go outside. The excited children immediately started picking up the newly-fallen snow and began playing with it. Some threw it around while others made snow angels. Meanwhile, a group of them, along with the teacher, began making a snowman.

Only 5 minutes had passed before one of the children, wearing soft mittens, came crying to the teacher about her wet, cold hands. Another child, who was making snow angels without snow pants on, came over crying with wet, soaked pants. While most of the children were running around enjoying the beautiful winter day, the children without proper winter gear were miserable. They were also sad because they couldn't continue playing along with the others. One of the teachers stepped out of the snow and walked over to stand by the building, where he kept the cold, wet children by his side. He continued to monitor the playing children from where he was standing, but felt frustrated that he couldn't interact with them in the snow. After a few more minutes, several more children without proper attire joined the "miserable group". At this point, the teachers decided that outside time had to be cut short and they called all the children to go inside. The children that were still happily playing were upset to have to go inside early, while the miserable ones couldn't wait. Once all the children came inside, the teachers could only hope that the wet children had some extra dry clothes in their cubbies to change into.

This story paints a very realistic picture of how miserable children can be if they don't have everything they need. It also makes the point that if some of the children are not prepared, it takes away from the other children's experiences as well. These situations cause unnecessary stress for everyone and throw important schedules off when events can't go as planned. It's so disheartening to see a child experience the misery of having freezing, cold, wet fingers, or wet clothes they can't change out of. In warmer climates, other "gear" may be necessary, including hats, swimsuits, towels, and sunblock. Whatever the case may be, make sure to provide everything your child needs, and their teachers can do the rest. Daycare can offer your child many things, but when it comes to their necessities, it's all up to you.

✶15.

Bonds and Bridges

Friendships and connections that build over time and can last a lifetime...

S tudies suggest that the bonds a child experiences with their first caregivers will determine their ability to trust and love throughout their lives. It makes sense, then, that having your child in an environment where they are loved and nurtured would help influence the type of individual they become.

Too often, daycare is considered as just a place for kids to go while their parents are at work, but is that really all it is?

While in daycare, children learn many things, but more important are the bonds and social skills they will develop with people outside of their family. They will develop close bonds with their caregivers and capture their hearts in so many ways. They will also develop first friendships that will often run deeper and last longer than parents would have ever expected. Most importantly, they will cultivate a sense of self and build bridges that will take them where they want to go in life. It's well known that the foundation is the strongest part of any structure. Children's daycare experiences will help them lay a strong foundation for a lifetime of loving, learning and success.

Love Connection

Childcare providers typically choose to be providers because they love and care about children. They can form very close bonds with the children in their care, especially when they begin caring for them as infants, and they get to experience a child growing up and reaching new milestones. Often times, parents don't realize just how strong these bonds are, or how hard it can be on the provider when a family's needs change and a child moves on.

A little girl had been attending a home daycare since she was six weeks old and had formed a very close bond with her daycare family. She was the same age as one of the provider's daughters and the two little girls had become best friends. The provider loved this bright, funny little girl and had been there to see her take her first steps, had watched her blow out her first birthday candle and, day by day, had watched her grow, learn, and develop new skills. The provider loved all of the kids in her care, but because of the friendship this child had with her daughter, she had an even closer bond with her. This child would often go to the provider's house for play dates, and visit on the weekends as well.

About a month after the little girl turned four, her mom told the provider she had a big announcement. She had received a promotion at work and her new job would be in a different city, about an hour away. They had decided to move and were extremely excited about their new future. The provider congratulated the mom and wished her luck in her new position, meanwhile wondering and worrying about how this was going to affect *her* life. The mom then casually added that she would be placing her daughter in the daycare at her work.

The provider, while happy for the family, suddenly felt sad. She couldn't imagine the thought of not seeing this child every day, and she knew that her daughter would be lost without her best friend. That night, as she broke down in tears, she couldn't help but wonder how the child was going to handle these big changes. Would she miss her daycare family as much as they would miss her? Would she be happy in her new daycare? Of course she knew families moved on for different reasons, and kids came and went, but she wondered if parents ever considered how hard it could be for providers to say goodbye to a child for whom they've cared for, for years and who had come to feel like their own.

Providers, just like parents, work tirelessly each day to care for and essentially help raise their daycare children. They become invested in your children's future and help to increase their chances of success. When a change makes it necessary for a child to leave our care, we are often left with a void to fill. As strange as it may sound, we will often mourn the loss of a child who we loved, formed a bond with and helped to develop, when he or she suddenly leaves our life for good. We realize, of course, there are no guarantees about how long a child will stay in daycare, but when they do move on, it means so much to us to know what we meant to that family. There's no greater compliment to a provider than to receive a Christmas card or an updated picture of a family that left our care, or a visit from them years later. It reminds us that that even though we were in their lives for only a limited time, we are still in their hearts and on their minds. Children have a special way of leaving marks on the hearts that they touch, and those early bonds and bridges that are formed can often last a lifetime.

• • • • •

When a child leaves a daycare, their absence can always be felt. The dynamics of the group always changes and their little face is definitely missed in the crowd.

• • • • •

Gone too Soon

A little boy started in our infant room at a few months old, and about a year later, he was about ready to move up to the Toddler Room. His parents were very friendly and we always had nice little chats here and there during pickup times. This child's mom was in her early 30s and seemed healthy and well. One day she came in limping and complained she wasn't feeling right. In the following weeks, her arms and legs got progressively weaker and she began going in for all kinds of tests.

A few weeks later, we received the horrific news that she was diagnosed with Lou Gehrig's disease, also known as ALS. We all knew what this meant, but I did not want to accept the fact that this parent (who was the same age as myself) with a young toddler had less than a year to live. We all hoped and prayed for the best. Within a few weeks, she became wheelchair-bound and was no longer able to work. At that point, I offered the services of myself and my staff, and told her and her husband we would help in any way we could.

It became difficult for the toddler's dad to bring him to daycare and pick him up, while tending to his wife at home, as well as continuing to work almost daily. We offered to begin picking up their son in the mornings, and dropping him off at the end of the day. This became our daily routine for the next several months, and during that time, we all developed a closer bond with this family. My bond grew especially close with his mom as I visited her weekly in the afternoons to offer my support, and sometimes bring her lunch.

By this time, she was aware she had only a few months left. When I asked her if there was anything else I could do for her, or any wishes I could fulfill, she said she had everything covered. The courage with which she accepted her fate, and her undeniable, unbroken faith in God, left me completely in awe. It seemed I was angrier at God than she was! She told me she was at peace knowing she had chosen the right daycare, and she knew we would continue to take good care of her son. It was all I could do to keep from falling apart, and I couldn't have thanked her more for her kind words, and what they meant to me. I told her that I knew she would be watching us from above, and we would make her proud by continuing to take good care of her son and help him develop to be his best. The certainty of knowing we were truly this child's second family now strengthened the bond his caregivers had already formed with him.

As I witnessed her passing days, watching her son run around while she sat, unable to hold him and interact with him, it continued to break my heart. But she remained strong; each time I would bring him home at the end of the day, her face would light up at the sight of him! Her son knew that his mom couldn't pick him up, so I would seat him in her lap, and he would stay there as long as a busy toddler can stay seated.

Although I knew a miracle cure was not going to save her, I was still not prepared for the morning I received the call that she had passed away. It had barely been 8 months since she first received her diagnosis. I sat and wept…for a mother who didn't get to experience the joy of watching her child grow, for a wife who didn't get to grow old with her husband, and for the loss of the daughter, sister and friend she was to others. I cried for the little boy who will not have his mother's love and presence in his life, and for a life taken away way too soon. Her strength and the dignity with which she carried herself until the very end will continue to inspire me and remind me to be so grateful for all that I have, for the rest of my life.

Choosing childcare is very much like choosing your extended family. It's a relationship that may last only as long as you need childcare, but the impression left behind, both for the providers and the families, can last forever.

• • • • •

I feel so blessed that since opening my center, so many of the teachers have remained with me for over ten years! This is phenomenal for the daycare business. It takes real passion for working with children to be able to last that long and still be going strong. When you find the right caregivers with that kind of dedication, they truly can become like a second family to your family.

• • • • •

My "Honey"

The cutest and earliest bond I've ever had the pleasure of watching form started with a little baby boy and a baby girl. These two enrolled at about the same time, and were both about four months old when they started in the Infant Room. The cribs were organized in a way that positioned the youngest infants' cribs in front, which meant these two babies had their cribs side by side. Two months went by….

One day, as I was checking on the Infant Room, I stepped into the napping area to peek at the sleeping babies. All were asleep except these two, who were laying in their cribs quietly. The next thing I saw gave me such a sweet surprise: These two little babies had reached their arms out through the crib slats and were holding each other's hands while smiling. They also had their heads tilted toward each other. It was one of the cutest things I've ever seen!

For the remainder of their time in the Infant Room, these two could always be found playing together and holding hands (they didn't let the other infants into their little circle). Eventually, they moved up to the Toddler Room together…

One evening, when the little girl's mother came to pick her up, the little girl ran over to her buddy, gave him a hug as they had always done, then added, "Bye, Honey." I happened to be in the room when this happened and was so amused! I wondered if she was perhaps imitating how her parents greeted each other. When I turned to the teacher with a surprised smile on my face, she stated, "They have been doing this for a while now." This went on for the next three years as they continued to move up in classrooms, and it was always so much fun to see them greet and say goodbye to each other. I ran into the little boy's mom a few years later after they had left my center and started kindergarten. She said the two of them were still having play dates together and were still calling each other "Honey".

There are many great moments children experience in a daycare setting with children their own age. Even in the early stages of their lives, they can begin forming bonds and creating strong friendships in ways we never would have thought possible.

Building a Bridge

A mom and dad enrolled their two children in a home daycare but were extremely apprehensive from the very beginning. The boys were two and four years old and had never been in daycare before. Mom and Dad admitted from the start that the boys had some behavioral problems which the parents had not dealt with consistently nor effectively. The daycare provider told the parents that it was never too late to start and she'd be happy to work with them. The parents were relieved to hear this since other providers, including their Sunday school teacher, had been hesitant to work with the boys on these issues.

The following week the boys started attending daycare and the provider immediately realized that the boys' "behavior problems" were due to the lack of structure, discipline and consistency in their days. A few weeks went by and many practices and routines were put into place by the daycare provider, which she urged the parents to continue at home. She found that the boys actually did very well when they were encouraged with positive reinforcement. They actually embraced the idea of having a "chores chart", and got quite competitive with each other…in a positive way. Soon Mom and Dad also noticed the positive changes in the boys' behavior and would look forward to speaking with the provider each night to ask questions and get more ideas for things to implement at home. The more the parents and the provider worked together, the more consistent the results became. The family was so grateful to have found someone willing to work with them, their situation and help guide them toward a successful outcome.

It's great when parents and daycare providers share a mutual respect for each other's positions in a child's upbringing. By establishing a bond between the provider and the parent, a strong, safe bridge gets formed for the child to confidently cross as he advances from one stage of development to the next. When both parties are equally committed and work together toward the building of that bridge, they can achieve the best possible results for the child.

16.

Home Away From Home

Where love and learning continue
and second families are found...

A child's first experiences of love, comfort, security, and a sense of belonging begin at home; therefore, it's important for a child's daycare setting to also feel that way. This is especially true for children that spend more waking hours at daycare than they do at home. When kids feel that sense of comfort, connection, and belonging, they have a better chance of succeeding. Not only will they adapt to their new environment more quickly, but they will be more receptive to learning and interacting with other children, and ready to thrive and accept what daycare has to offer.

Daycare can offer a wealth of knowledge and experiences, and offer diversity to children that might not be exposed to it otherwise. It can also teach them to grow and develop a broader sense of their world. In the end, whether it's a home daycare or a center, children who are happy and comfortable in their daycare

environment will excitedly look forward to each new day, knowing that friends, fun and new experiences await. Some children will like their daycare so much, they will cry when it's time to go home, and some will even ask if they can go to daycare on the weekends.

When this happens, and it does happen occasionally, it's a great indication that your child loves their daycare and it's an even greater compliment to your child's provider. As hard as this can be for parents to understand, they shouldn't take it personally. Instead, they should celebrate the fact that they made a great choice for their child! Finding a place where their child is happy and eager to go to everyday should offer parents tremendous peace of mind that their child is in good hands.

● ● ● ● ●

Some kids arrive at daycare extremely early and are often waiting in driveways and parking lots for daycare to open. Many daycares offer special accommodations for these children and let them go back to sleep in quiet areas or wear their pajamas to daycare and get dressed later.

● ● ● ● ●

A Kiss for Everyone

Kids that attend home daycares often end up feeling like part of the daycare provider's family, which is why many parents actually choose home daycares for their children. The kids can become very comfortable in the provider's home and the provider's kids can become like their siblings...

A little girl had been attending a home daycare since she was three months old. This little girl loved and adored the daycare provider, her children and her husband, and they loved and adored her as well. As she grew older, she started giving hugs and kisses to everyone at daycare each morning upon arrival, and she would do the same thing each evening upon leaving. Her parents were overjoyed to know that she was so loved by her daycare family and felt so comfortable in their home.

One morning, the daycare provider's husband was packing his lunch and getting ready to leave for the day. He walked over to his wife and kissed her goodbye, then kissed each of his daughter's goodbye. As he started to head for the door, the little girl jumped up and ran after him screaming, "me, me!" He turned to look at her and there she stood with her little face looking up at him as if to say, *Aren't you forgetting someone?* The provider's husband smiled at her, then leaned down and kissed the top of her head. She patted her head, smiled, and toddled back over to the group, completely satisfied that she hadn't been excluded from the goodbye kisses. The same thing happened the next day, and the next, and soon the provider's husband just knew to include her in his morning routine of goodbye kisses, or he would be very loudly reminded to do so!

As a parent, knowing that your provider loves, cares for and treats your child like one of their own makes going to work so much easier. When your child is excited each morning and can't wait to leave for daycare or is less than thrilled to go home at night, know that you have done a great job finding a place where your child feels right at home. Many parents worry about the long hours their children spend in daycare, but if your children are loved, well cared for and comfortable in their environment, then why worry? You are doing your job and providing for your family while your kids are growing, learning social and academic skills, and forming lasting friendships. It truly can be a win-win situation!

No, Not Yet!

I was sitting in the office early one afternoon, when I heard a child crying in the lobby. As the center's director, I know many of the children's cries by sound but I couldn't figure out this time who seemed to be so sad. When the cry turned into a loud, high-pitched wail, I became more concerned and jumped to my feet to investigate the situation.

As I opened the office door, I saw a parent kneeling in front of her child, trying unsuccessfully to put on his mittens and hat. My concerns immediately turned to joy as I listened to the child say, "I don't want to go!" over and over again. This child had never previously attended daycare and had recently begun attending our morning preschool program which ended at 12:30. He was quiet at first but before long, he got into a regular routine and began making friends. As he came to feel more at home in his new environment and really started to enjoy himself, he would often cry at pickup time and beg Mom to let him stay a little longer. That day, however, his tantrum hit a whole new level.

I turned to his mom with a big smile and told her that I felt bad for the tantrum she was having to deal with, but I also couldn't be happier! She smiled back and admitted that although she'd love to see him get excited about going home, she was glad he was so happy at daycare that he didn't want to leave. It was truly a heartwarming moment to know that my staff and I had created a warm and loving environment where kids felt comfortable, accepted, and truly at home.

As luck would have it, the mother ended up getting her work hours increased, and he began attending the center full time. We were all so thrilled, and he... well, he was ecstatic!

When a child feels completely comfortable and "at home" in an environment, it should be easy to sense and see in their actions. A happy, smiling child that doesn't want to go home at the end of the day should give you peace of mind knowing you've succeeded in finding the right place.

The Wish

Life has become so busy these days that it's become a constant struggle to maintain family practices that were so common years ago. Having dinner with one's family is one of those important bonding times that, for many, has gone to the wayside. These days, kids will eat in the living room, in their room, on the go, and just about anywhere else except at the table with their family. Even those that may eat as a family may find it more distressful at times than enjoyable.

As a parent and a daycare provider, I now get to determine the importance of these practices both in my home and at work. Mealtimes at home, as well as in daycare, can be a time for socializing, bonding and learning important self-help skills. Children can practice family-style dining, passing bowls of food around, and learn to serve themselves and pour from pitchers – sometimes with help. They can try new foods, discover their health benefits, and discuss what makes up a healthy meal. They can also practice good table manners during this time. Some centers have meals catered, where each child will get a pre-portioned tray of food, while others have cooks on staff preparing meals on site.

At many centers, children recite a wish before they eat. A very popular one goes like this: "We wish for peace, love, happiness and food for all the people in the whole world. Thank you for our food." Kids will sometimes learn to express this wish in sign language as well. Reciting this wish teaches the children to appreciate what they are given and to extend compassion to others. During mealtimes, children have the opportunity to chat with each other, laugh and enjoy social time around a table, just like a family would at home. This is a time when staff can slow down and enjoy some one-on-one time with the children, asking them to share about their weekends or anything else that's important to them. (Be careful of what they see and hear at home; many times *we* get to hear about it too!) They learn to respect adults and caregivers by asking to be excused when they are done and to follow a routine of cleaning up their own spot and washing up. Sharing a meal at daycare can teach children so many things and give those who don't typically get this experience some valuable bonding and socialization time.

Many children will tell us what their meals are like at home, and many involve kids eating on the go on their way to evening activities or in front of a TV. While enjoying a family-like mealtime experience at daycare, they learn and benefit from all that sharing a meal has to offer.

• • • • •

One day while having breakfast around the table with my daycare kids, one of the kids noticed I was drinking coffee. She cutely stated that her mom also loved to drink coffee and so did her dad. The other kids quickly chimed in with their parents' favorite drinks and one little boy innocently looked at me and said, "My dad loves beer the best but sometimes on the weekends, he loves whiskey."

• • • • •

Turbulent Times

A little boy had been attending a home daycare since birth and had always felt very happy and secure with his daycare family. At about the age of three, the daycare provider started to notice changes in the child's behavior as he became very attached to her and would cry when it was time to go home. This initially concerned the provider but, since this child had many friends in daycare, she assumed that he was probably just unhappy about having to leave his friends each day, so she didn't really give it much more thought.

Soon after, the child started to ask the provider odd questions that didn't make sense. He would ask her if he could come to daycare on the weekends, if he could sleep over at her house and he started to question the age he would be when daycare would come to an end. The provider again began to worry that something was wrong, so she decided to talk it over with the child's parents.

The next day when Mom came to pick up her son, as usual the boy ran and hid and didn't want to go home. The provider felt this was a perfect opportunity to ask Mom if everything was alright. After a silent pause, Mom explained that she and her husband had been going through a really hard time for the past several months and he had just recently moved out and filed for divorce. She also stated that she felt horribly about her son crying a lot during this trying time, and that just recently, he had begun asking to come to daycare even in the evenings. The provider, now able to understand the child's behavior more clearly, was saddened by this news and wondered why she hadn't been informed sooner.

Many times families will go through tough times due to sickness of a family member, divorce, or some other circumstance. These are the times when communication becomes very important between parents and providers to address the behavioral changes the children may be experiencing. A child's daycare should be a place of love and comfort, and daycare providers need to be informed when drastic changes are occurring at home in order to support and help the children transition through these rough times. Having a second family and a home away from home often allows needed comfort and support to children when they need it most.

17.

Memories and Milestones

It's the memories we make through life's journeys that matter most...

ost childcare providers will have many wonderful stories of children they've cared for through the years, and will have been undeniably, greatly touched by them. Children that have come into our lives leave their own unique imprint on our hearts, and bittersweet memories of the huge milestones we have helped them achieve.

Childcare may not always offer the benefits of other careers but, as providers, we feel so privileged to be a part of children's lives. Parents don't always realize that while they are choosing us to care for and teach their children, they are also selflessly sharing their child with us and allowing us to be a part of their lives. As we witness children reach new milestones throughout their time with us, their great moments become our great moments as well. We get to see babies take their first wobbly steps, hear their first spoken words, see first friendships form

and, years later, see those same kids climb the big stairs of the bus on their first day of kindergarten.

While each child leaves us with many cherished memories, we hope they leave our care with many fond, fun-filled memories of their own…memories of a childhood full of friends, adventures, love, laughter, learning and carefree days that to them seemed never-ending. We often don't realize until years later just how fondly they look back on their daycare years and how much they actually remember. We occasionally have families visit us years later and mention how their children still talk about their daycare days. Occasionally, we will run into a teenager who's hardly recognizable, who ends up noticing us and blurting out, "Hey, remember me? I came to your daycare!"

One of the Firsts

When I first opened my daycare center, two of the first five children that enrolled was a three-year-old boy and his infant sibling. Through the years, the young boy had his ups and downs, and my dedicated staff worked with him on his occasional outbursts and stubborn moments. He and my daughter were the same age, so they ended up attending Kindergarten at the same school. (I still have the picture of the first day he and my daughter went to school together in the daycare van.)

One morning, when it was time for him to be driven to school, he was in one of his stubborn and angry moods and refused to leave the daycare. It took two teachers to finally get him into the van and, when they arrived at school, he refused to get out. The teacher got out of the van and tried to encourage and assist him out, but he wouldn't budge. Despite his little size, he was a very strong boy, so she didn't want to take a chance on hurting herself by carrying him. She decided she needed help and told the boy she would be calling the Principal out to come get him if he didn't get out on his own. Still nothing. He probably figured it was just an empty threat. A few minutes later, the Principal appeared and said a few words to him while he was still in the van. She then gave her hand to him, and he calmly stepped out and walked into the school with her.

Years went by, and his time with us at the daycare was coming to an end. He was in seventh grade now, and soon would be turning 13, the legal cutoff age for school-agers in daycare centers. During this time, the other children in middle school at our daycare didn't think they should still be in daycare, nor did they like getting picked up by a daycare van. They had requested the teacher pick them up behind the school in an inconspicuous spot where their friends couldn't see them enter the daycare van. Ironically, this boy, who had acted like he didn't want to be at daycare when he was younger and had given staff such a hard time, was now the only one among the middle school students who didn't mind. He felt fine about getting picked up by the van *in front* of the school, and would frequently announce to everyone that "daycare is cool".

We all knew that once he left, the place would never be the same, and it wasn't; meanwhile his mother had two more children, so his younger siblings continued to attend and one of them still does. One afternoon, as I was leaving the center, I heard someone yell, "Bye, Rita" from the preschool room. I yelled back, "Bye" and continued walking out the door, wondering who the tall man in the preschool room was and how he knew my name. Suddenly I stopped in my tracks and realized who it was. It was the little boy who was now in 11th grade, taller than a beanstalk with a voice deeper than Barry White's. He'd come in with his mom to pick up his little brother. I ran back in and gave him a hug (on my tippy toes) and, squeezing his (partially bearded) cheeks, I told him, "To me, you will always be that little boy I remember."

Some children will spend over a decade with the same provider, and they may end up having to say goodbye as a teenager, but will likely never be forgotten. And what's so rewarding for a provider is when they are told by those children, if they are lucky enough to see them again, that they, too, are still remembered. This child went on to tell me how he loved his daycare days, and they were some of the best days in his life. I never thought, of all the kids that entered my daycare, this one, who acted like he was "too cool" at times, would be the one who loved it the most.

Season of Memories

Christmas time is a season where we reflect on the year that's coming to an end and look forward to the New Year ahead. A home daycare provider had started a tradition many years earlier with her daycare families and to this day, the tradition continues. Each year, on the last day of daycare before Christmas, she would hand out special and unique ornaments to each of the children. She put a lot of thought into the ornaments that she selected for each child, choosing symbols of the milestones each one accomplished and things they had been interested in. Her favorites were the tiny blue and pink booties for the babies' first Christmas, inscribed with their names as well as the year. Many little boys were given tractor and train ornaments, and for the girls, she especially loved giving them fluffy pink ballerinas and princess crowns. As the children grew older and started school, they often were given chalkboard ornaments covered in colorful letters and numbers to celebrate the many things that they were now learning in school.

The daycare provider loved this tradition and each year, as she decorated her own tree, she would think of all the children she cared for throughout the years and wonder if they were hanging their ornaments and remembering those happy times as well. She also loved receiving Christmas photo cards her daycare parents would send of their children, which she proudly displayed on her mantle. She loved seeing pictures of toothless eight- and nine-year-olds who she had cared for as babies, and knowing that she was still in their families' hearts and minds.

Choosing to be a daycare provider is essentially offering to join many parents on their journey to help raise their children. Providers, like many, may end their job at 5:00, but their dedication and compassion for their daycare kids continues beyond that. Daycare providers will worry when their daycare kids are sick, they will celebrate their birthdays and achievements, and they will continue to wonder how the kids they once provided care for are doing. While the kids may only be in the provider's care for a short period of time, they will be in their thoughts and memories long after that.

Where is my Sister?

Every child is special in their own unique way; however, there are always those that leave lasting impressions for a lifetime. I had a boy who started attending my center as an infant who had recently been adopted from a Russian orphanage. When his parents signed him up, they explained that he had suffered developmental, social and emotional delays due to the treatment he received in the orphanage. He struggled with eating, receiving physical affection and interacting with others. The teachers put in a lot of extra time and hard work to help him get to his appropriate level of development. Many times, this proved to be quite challenging, given the nature of his delays, his never-ending curiosity and the amount of exuberant energy (and strength) he was blessed with. When he moved up to the Toddler Room, the teachers were chasing him almost constantly to keep him from climbing everything in sight, from the furniture to the walls!

Throughout his years at the center, the teachers saw and were encouraged by the strides he made in his ability to communicate, focus and extend compassion to others. When another child was sad, he would turn and look at the teacher and start "fake crying" since he thought he should be sad too; he did it with such emotion that you couldn't help but laugh and adore him that much more! He would give hugs to his friends, and when he accidentally bumped them, he would yell out, "I sorry, I sorry!" an inch from their face. Once when his classroom door was open, which led to the Infant Room, he stood and peeked over the gate that blocked the doorway. When he noticed another friend from his class visiting her little sister in the Infant Room, he quickly began to shout while jumping up and down excitedly, "I want to see my sister too! I want to see my sister too!" While holding the gate, and continuing to jump with all the excitement, energy and strength he could muster, he broke the gate loose and came crashing down to the floor with it! His teachers, startled that he was able to knock the gate loose, quickly ran to his side and lifted him up. He wasn't hurt, but instead was smiling with a big open grin that showed his teeth (luckily all intact). So happy he made it into the room, he immediately began searching for his baby sister. His teachers couldn't help but laugh before telling him, "Honey, you don't have a sister."

All children can be challenging in their own ways. A quality provider welcomes these challenges and creates learning opportunities to benefit the child. Taking the time to discover children's individual needs is key to helping them reach their full potential. The unique experiences my staff and I shared with this boy during the four years we had him left us with fond memories that we still laugh and reminisce about almost a decade later. I still get a smile on my face every time I think of him and I wonder how and what he's doing these days…

•   •   •   •   •

A group of elementary kids were crying in the school-age room at daycare on their last day of school. It was a sight to see these

11-year-old children huddled up in corners of the classroom bawling their eyes out. When the teacher asked them what was wrong, they replied they were sad (and scared) about having to start middle school in the fall, and were already missing their elementary school and the friends that would be going to different schools. It didn't take long before their tears turned to non-stop fun and activities as they enjoyed their "end of the school year party" at their daycare. Daycare offers many comforts to children and despite other changes in their life, they can count on the security and consistency they have come to expect there.

• • • • •

Pride on the High Dive

A little boy and his brother had been attending a home daycare for several years. They had learned many things and reached many milestones during that time, and the provider had always taken pictures along the way to share their many accomplishments with their parents. Both boys had taken swimming lessons every summer, and the older boy was soon going to learn to dive.

A few weeks before the start of summer, the mom found out she was going to have another baby and decided to take the summer off to spend with her children. The provider was happy for the family, yet disappointed that she wouldn't be spending time with the boys that summer. What further saddened her was the fact that the boys were going to start school in the fall, so this would end up being their final farewell. She was going to miss them, but providers get used to bonding with children for a short time and then having to let them go.

A few weeks into the summer, the daycare provider was sitting at the edge of the swimming pool overseeing a group of kids when she heard her name called. She looked around but couldn't figure out who was trying to get her attention. She heard it again and still could not figure out where the voice was coming from or who was calling her. A few minutes later, she saw the mother of the two boys she used to care for. The mother told the provider that her older son was on the high dive and he was screaming for her to watch! The provider and her daycare kids walked over to the fence that separated the big and little pools and looked up at the high dive. There stood the older brother, who, upon seeing his spectators, did a perfect dive into the pool and came up seconds later with a huge smile on his face. "I did it! I did it!" he screamed, and all the kids cheered him on by clapping and jumping up and down. The daycare provider was so proud of the boy for what he had learned so quickly and even more overjoyed that he wanted so badly to show her.

Many lasting memories and milestones can come out of a good quality daycare experience and the lessons that are learned can serve a child throughout his life. Remember, when your children leave a daycare that has contributed positively to their lives, they are probably leaving a lasting impression on their providers as well. When kids leave, providers are often left wondering how they are doing or if they have further developed any of the skills providers had first introduced them to. It's always so heartwarming to see children years later and realize that we have a special place in their hearts too.

18.

What Your Child Walks Away With...

*They come to us as little ones and leave us
with greater minds and hearts.*

When your child has been through a wonderful daycare journey, you will see the huge impact of that positive experience on his or her life. When we think of our own children, and how they've grown through the years, we can see the effect daycare has had on them and how priceless the influence of their experience has been. We have seen them learn and grow in ways that have amazed us, and have left us with no doubt that a quality childcare experience was the foundation for that outcome.

When children are exposed to other children, especially at a young age, they excel and develop skills that come later for some children that stay at home. Their development of social, verbal, and academic skills can set them ahead of children with no preschool experience. These skills are very important for kindergarten readiness, so it's to a child's advantage to establish them early.

We all want the best for our children, but it's not always easy to know what that is with certainty. When you make the right daycare choice, you will see it in the smiles and excitement that will greet you at the end of each day. You will hear it through their constant chatter when they share all about the fun activities and learning they are experiencing. Most of all, you will feel it as they express in many ways all the love they have come to feel and understanding they have gained about themselves and the world they live in. Although the thought of daycare may have been terrifying at first, we hope through these stories, you will discover what a wonderful experience it can be.

• • • • •

Once my three-year-old son yelled at his older sister when she got up to leave the dinner table, "You didn't ask to be excused!" I was so surprised and proud at the same time of how serious he was about following the rules he learned at daycare.

• • • • •

BFF'S

Many years ago I was working in an Infant Room in a daycare center and was assigned four babies to care for throughout the day as my "primary care group". All four babies were little girls with birthdays that were only days apart. I loved watching these little girls interact as they smiled and babbled at each other and even held hands at the table while they were being fed. It was amazing to see friendships start at such a young age!

As time went by, the girls moved up to the Toddler Room and they remained very close and often played with only each other. Through the years, they remained best friends, going to one another's birthday parties and over time, even their moms became close friends. Eventually, they all left the daycare and went to school, but they always kept in touch. Through the years, I have received many birthday invitations, first communion announcements and even prom and homecoming pictures of the girls. Last year, I received four graduation announcements for the girls and was amazed by how fast time had flown by and also that their families were still including me in their lives and updating me on their successes. First friendships really can last a lifetime and knowing that I was there when it all began made it extra rewarding to me as a daycare provider.

Many first friendships and close bonds will come out of a great daycare situation. By exposing your children to other kids at a young age you are also helping them to learn many life lessons that they might not have otherwise been exposed to. Friends are an important part of every child's life and when they have friends they look forward to seeing each day, daycare can be a very happy place to be!

Please Stop, I Don't Like That!

Early communication skills allow children to express themselves without having to get physical. It's very common for children in their toddler years to push, scratch and bite each other as a form of communicating their feelings. A toddler teacher cleverly came up with a very effective way of teaching toddlers how to communicate those feelings of frustration in a different way.

This toddler teacher taught her toddlers, ranging from 16 months to 33 months, to say the phrase, "Please stop, I don't like that," while they pound a hand into their open palm. As she continuously practiced this with them, the toddlers caught on quickly! Those who could speak would say the phrase while doing the hand motions, while those who couldn't would just do the hand motions. When this technique really caught on in the classroom, the amount of biting, hitting and pushing drastically decreased. "It was a sight to see," as the teacher described, and even the youngest ones, who didn't speak or use the hand motions, knew what it meant when they saw and heard others around them, or were being told themselves. One parent mentioned how well her two-year-old daughter ended up applying this practice so creatively at home…

When the mom would ask her to pick up her toys, eat her food, get ready for bed, or any other reasonable request, her toddler would look at her with a very straight face and say with a firm tone, "Please stop, I don't like that," as she pounded her hand into her palm. The first time this happened, the mom was surprised and amused at her toddler's response which showed how much her child was learning at daycare. Eventually, it got to the point where this toddler would use this phrase for almost anything she didn't want to do. The mother had to explain to her child that this phrase (and hand gesture) was meant to stop someone from hurting or bothering her, not to get her out of doing things expected of her. The teacher got a kick out of hearing this, and didn't realize how well her toddlers would understand and be able to fully apply this concept. She was happy to see they were practicing it outside the daycare, even if it *was* being a bit abused.

We sometimes underestimate what our children can learn at such a young age. This example reminds us of how incredibly smart children are and their innate ability to apply concepts in their own creative way, above and beyond how they were taught. Repetition with words and actions is key in teaching children new methods and ideas (which also reminds us to always be aware of what we are constantly saying and doing in front of them). The skill of communication, especially at such a young age, is such an important one to have.

• • • • •

A teacher asked her three-year-old student to please go hang up her coat. The little girl looked at her teacher then continued to color her picture. When the teacher asked her again, she was once again ignored by the child. After asking for the third time with no response, the teacher said to her, "If you asked me to do something, I would listen to you and do it." Upon hearing this, the child smirked at her teacher then asked in an ever so sweet voice, "Please go hang up my coat."

• • • • •

Queen of the Daycare

Kids learn many important life lessons just by being exposed to other children and being in daycare. One very interesting dynamic is that when children who don't have siblings are placed in daycare, they soon realize that being Queen at home does not mean you are Queen of the daycare. These children learn very quickly what it means to share, take turns, compromise and communicate.

A stay-at-home mom decided to place her three-year-old daughter in a nearby daycare center for three days a week. She wanted some time to herself to run errands and she felt that the child needed more social interaction and time around other children, particularly having recently noticed some troubling behaviors when around other children and friends. She thought if she was in daycare, she would be exposed to kids her own age and learn more appropriate behaviors from them. Since this child was used to getting her own way and had never had to share a single thing in her life, her favorite word was "mine".

On the first day of daycare, the teachers were delighted to see a smiling cute little blonde girl in pig tails walk through the door. By the end of the day, the teachers realized why Mom needed a break and some time to herself! The little girl had screamed "mine" constantly and had tried to take toys away from almost every child in the room. She had thrown huge tantrums, bitten a child that wouldn't hand over a doll, and spit her food out and demanded something different when lunch didn't quite suit her picky little princess palate. The teachers realized very quickly that this child was an "only child" and that she probably had mom and dad running in circles at home to please her. She was used to being given anything she wanted and the parents' lives clearly revolved around this child's every need and desire. The teachers had seen many kids like her before and knew very well how being in daycare would soon change this situation.

Daycare is the perfect place to expose a child without siblings to a world full of little chairs where no one has a throne. Though it may be tough at first, and they may take a little longer to adjust, kids eventually learn important life lessons like sharing, taking turns and using words to communicate their feelings effectively without becoming frustrated. "Only" children generally end up loving daycare and making many close friends that substitute as siblings.

Children learn about appropriate behavior and social skills by watching and interacting with other children. One of the greatest things an 'only' child takes away from daycare is the experience of being part of a team and learning how to work with others. Exposing children to experiences that broaden their view of their world will prepare them for what lies ahead and help them realize, whether in daycare or in school, there are no Kings and Queens, just friends.

Give Him Space

One day my son, who was four at that time, was playing with a child that had recently been diagnosed with a mild form of autism. This child had been attending our daycare for quite some time and after his diagnosis, his teachers had implemented many practices and techniques that the child could use when he needed a" break". The other children understood that he occasionally needed some space and learned to work with him and around him, and whenever the child wanted, he was warmly welcomed into the other children's circle of play. At times, when he became really upset, he would uncontrollably and unintentionally push or scratch a child that was in his way.

On this particular day, while the two were playing, the child suddenly had an outburst and scratched my son's face, leaving four deep, long, bloody scratches on his cheek. My son was shaken by the incident and I was uncertain and concerned about how he would deal with it. These two had become good friends and I knew my son enjoyed playing with him, so I hoped this incident wouldn't change that. Later that night, I asked him how he felt about what had happened and his response left me choked up and speechless. He said, "Mom, I know he didn't mean it. He needed a break and I should've left him alone when I saw he was getting upset. It's ok, I still like playing with him." At that moment, I was so full of pride for the kind of (little) man he had already become.

I saw another great example of the empathy he had learned when he was turning six and making plans for his birthday party. He wanted to invite three boys, whose parties he had recently gone to, plus one other boy. I had recently met this other boy and his mom at their school Halloween party and his mom had informed me at that time that her son had ADHD, attention deficit hyperactivity disorder. When my son passed out his invitations, this mom called me, almost in tears, to thank me for inviting her son, who hadn't been invited to any of the other birthday parties yet that year. She also mentioned that her son talked about my son a lot, and she was so grateful that he had made a friend in school. I was so touched, and proudly told her that I had nothing to do with the friends he chose to invite, and that my son considered her son to be one of his "best friends". I knew I owed much of his ability to feel compassion toward others, and acceptance of their differences without judgment, to the diversity he was exposed to at daycare and to all he was taught by his caring and compassionate daycare teachers.

The child who was diagnosed with autism was such a sweet and loving child. We, as staff, felt so very fortunate to have been blessed with him in our lives, and still reminisce about him. In many situations, we can learn as much from, if not more than, the children we're teaching. It's all about how the situation is presented and accepted. Learning to accept diversity and seeing the beauty that each individual has to offer is one of the greatest lessons a child can receive at an early age.

●　●　●　●　●

A child was asked by his parent, as they were leaving daycare, if he was a good boy or bad boy that day. The child replied, "I'm not bad. I just forget to use my listening ears sometimes. But today I had them on." The way a thought or feeling can be changed just by using different words can make the difference between success and failure. Teaching a child new ways to consider their behavior gives them ownership of it instead of having to label themselves as one thing or another.

●　●　●　●　●

Acknowledgements

To my husband Tom: Thank you for taking me away from Los Angeles and bringing me to sanity, and for always believing in me and supporting my vision. Without you, my dream of running a daycare would have remained a dream. You will always be my best friend and soul mate for life. (No more going to bed alone while I stay up writing.) I will love you forever.

To all the current families and the ones who came before: Thank you for entrusting and placing your children's care under my guidance and for sharing their smiles and hugs which has added SO MUCH joy and love to my life.

To those who have worked at Pumpkin Patch that have since moved on but left a little piece of themselves behind: Thank you for being an intricate part of the amazing environment you've helped create which I am so very proud of! I am blessed to have had all of you in my and my children's lives. I cannot express enough gratitude for all that you have given to the children that have walked through our daycare doors for the past 13 years.

To the current team at Pumpkin Patch, some of whom have been with me since the beginning... Mr. Richie, Mr. Mark, Ms. Ugaso, Ms. Kadra, Ms. Amino, Ms. Fatima, Ms. Fathiya, Ms. Mana, Ms. Megan, Ms. Kim, Ms. Amber and Ms. Pat: Every bit of what you do every day is what makes our place so great and makes it ROCK! It's not every day a work team becomes like a second family to each other, which is what we will continue to be. Thank you , thank you, thank you from the bottom of my heart, for all your patience, for all your gifts and mainly for truly wanting the best for every child you care for everyday. I am humbled by your passion and dedication to working with kids.

To my children Zakia, Tommy, Sophia and Christian: You have been my greatest lessons and my greatest loves, and will continue to be. Without you, daycare wouldn't have been necessary and neither would this journey have been traveled. At the end of the day, it's all about what we continue to give to each other that matters—unconditional love, laughter, comfort, warmth, sometimes madness, and an everlasting bond. Please always love each other as you do now… in the end, family is all that matters.

To my Editor (and sister) Ani Missakian Cole—my favorite perfectionist nut: Thank you for pouring your heart and soul into this project. You polished our rough stone into a brilliant diamond and taught me so many things in the process! You are one of my greatest teachers and I lovingly thank you for all you have brought to my life.

To my co-author Becky: WE DID IT! Thank you for continuing to push me even when I didn't want to be pushed any further. We have come to the end of our 3-year-long dream only to wake and find it's not a dream anymore but our new exciting reality! As much as we drove each other crazy, we also made a pretty good team and kept each other inspired—*that* we will always do for each other.

To my right-hand woman and Assistant director Amanda: I have learned so much from watching you work and I am so lucky to have you in my life. Thank you for always acknowledging how far we've come, how many anniversaries Pumpkin Patch has celebrated (you remembered even when my husband didn't), and for continuing to always be so passionate in your work with children. We're each other's yin and yang. (We *must* be to have been able to share such a small office for almost 12 years!) Thank you for all the love and support through the years and for the wonderful friendship we formed along the way.

Finally, to Morgan James Publishing: We thank you for believing in our project as much as we did!

—Rita

First and foremost I would like to thank all of the parents that have placed their trust and faith in me and allowed me to care for their most valuable possessions, their children. Each child that I have had the privilege of caring for has taught me something, and those lessons have inspired me to teach and share life's little learning moments with others!

Next I would like to thank our editor Ani Cole, for all of her hard work and dedication to this project. I learned many things from you about grammar, hydration, sleep, and why it's important to eat the core of a pineapple. Although a grueling process at times, we ended up with a finished product to be proud of and for that I sincerely thank you.

And where do I begin to thank my co-author Rita? You frazzled my nerves and drove me nuts in every way humanly possible but at the end of each day you always came through and I truly appreciate that. We have pushed, inspired, consoled and encouraged each other through this long and winding process but, most importantly, we never allowed the other to give up and that's what true friends do. We took a leap of faith together blindly into a place we had never been, and look at us now! Thanks for trusting me and jumping when I said "jump!"

Finally, thanks Kevin and Sally, you're lifesavers!

—Becky

CPSIA information can be obtained
at www.ICGtesting.com
Printed in the USA
BVHW072304180619
551377BV00001B/2/P

9 781630 473136